"This book is a good read for all Ameri... ample for all of us in her remarkable ca... book, she provides an instructive and i... plays in democracy. She convincingly a... leaders alike, play the crucial role in ensuring fairness, integrity, and transparency to preserve and protect our country."

—The Honorable Lee Hamilton

"Whether it has been in the political, governmental, academic, or personal world, it was always clear to me that Jill Long Thompson has made the effort to comport herself with the highest standards of ethics, integrity, and character. Now she makes a strong, timely, and convincing argument on why we as a country need to refocus on these standards, and how we can do that. Not only should we expect more from our political and business leaders, but we need to challenge ourselves, in our personal behavior, to do better as well. The future of our 'experiment in democracy' depends on what we decide and what we do."

—The Honorable Paul Helmke

"*The Character of American Democracy* is a must-read for every person who values the ideals upon which our nation was founded. There has never been a more urgent time for us to look in the mirror and candidly assess how we are running our country. It is an awesome responsibility we all share. *The Character of American Democracy* provides us insight and guidance on how do it better."

—The Honorable Marcy Kaptur

"*The Character of American Democracy* a must-read for everyone who cares about civility and ethics in politics and public affairs."

—Charles Taylor, Managing Director, Bowen Center for
Public Affairs, Ball State University

"Dr. Long Thompson's book makes a persuasive case for not only the importance of ethics in leadership, but also the critical role that laws and policies play in supporting and encouraging such ethical behavior."

—Sam Berger, Vice President of Democracy and Government
Reform at the Center for American Progress

THE CHARACTER OF
AMERICAN
DEMOCRACY

THE CHARACTER OF AMERICAN DEMOCRACY

Preserving Our Past, Protecting Our Future

—ɯɯ—

JILL LONG THOMPSON

INDIANA UNIVERSITY PRESS

This book is a publication of

Indiana University Press
Office of Scholarly Publishing
Herman B Wells Library 350
1320 East 10th Street
Bloomington, Indiana 47405 USA

iupress.indiana.edu

Manufactured in the United States of America

Cataloging information is available from the Library of Congress.

ISBN 978-0-253-05042-7 (hardback)
ISBN 978-0-253-05043-4 (paperback)
ISBN 978-0-253-05044-1 (ebook)

1 2 3 4 5   24 23 22 21 20

Our democracy is not a product but a continual process. It is preserved not by monuments but deeds. Sometimes it needs refining; sometimes it needs amending; sometimes it needs defending. Always, it needs improving.

And character is integral to its success.

THE HONORABLE LEE H. HAMILTON

CONTENTS

Acknowledgments   ix

Foreword by Marcy Kaptur   xi

Introduction: Ethics Are Fundamental to Democracy   *1*

1   American Character   *9*

2   Decision-Making with Character   *39*

3   The Habit of Leading with Character   *51*

4   Ethics and Democracy   *63*

5   Democracy, Ethics, and Capitalism   *89*

6   The American's Character   *103*

Conclusion: Strength of Character, Strength of Union   *123*

Notes   *125*

Index   *139*

ACKNOWLEDGMENTS

THIS PROJECT HAS BEEN A labor of love, not just because of the topic but because of family, friends, and colleagues who provided insight, expertise, and support.

My husband, Don, has been an incredible partner and gentle critic throughout the writing of this book. As always, my parents, Jean and Roger, and brothers, Mike and Mick, were very supportive, and my cousin Cheryl Franks provided invaluable guidance on the subtitle and cover design.

Ed Feigenbaum, Michelle Livinghouse, Christian Sautter, and Inga Smulkstys were instrumental in helping to establish the focus and parameters for this work. As I wrote the first draft, their early and continued feedback helped clarify both my thinking and writing.

I sincerely thank Idie Kesner, Dean of the Kelley School of Business, for her support of this project. And Gary Dunham at Indiana University Press provided exceptional direction on the purpose and scope of this work. I am very grateful to be a part of Indiana University, an institution and community that, many years ago, provided opportunities that changed the trajectory of my life.

The knowledge, insight, judgment, and support of my friends and colleagues Bonnie Brownlee, Kelly Eskew, Timothy Fort, Bruce Jaffee, Wendy Laguarda, Dubos J. Masson, Mary Meagher, William Meaux, Catherine Noe, Joseph Miller, Richard Painter, Charles Rawls, Mark Sauter, Greg Udell, and Wayne Winston were remarkable. Because their analyses and suggestions were so helpful and constructive, I did not even mind the resulting revisions and rewrites. I also appreciate the support that Clayola Brown provided to this work. Law student Dakota Coates was very helpful in reviewing all the citations for accuracy and clarity, and Michelle Curry provided the technical guidance for preparing and submitting the final draft.

I am very honored by and appreciative of the support of Senator Maria Cantwell, Congressman Lee Hamilton, Mayor Paul Helmke, Congresswoman Marcy Kaptur, Congressman John Lewis, and Secretary Leon Panetta.

This book would not have happened without the help and support of these family members and friends, and I thank them for all they did to make writing this book so enjoyable. I think this work is important to our political process and have made every effort to ensure that there are no errors or oversights. If there are any shortcomings, I accept complete responsibility and want to make clear that my friends and colleagues only improved the final product.

FOREWORD

THE HONORABLE MARCY KAPTUR

THIS BOOK IS A MUST-READ for every person who values the ideals upon which our nation was founded. Liberty. Equality. Justice. For all.

Jill offers a unique perspective on the relationship between ethics and our representative democracy. She makes a convincing case that the democratic process is undermined when either citizenry or leadership engages in unethical behavior. We all have a meaningful role to play in shaping America's future. In America, every voice matters. The character we demonstrate as individuals will determine how successful we are as a nation.

I have known the author for more than thirty years. How well I remember her commitment to strengthening ethics rules for members of Congress. What I especially like about this work is the clarity with which she presents basic ethics principles and then relates them to democracy and capitalism. I believe that anyone who reads this book will see clearly why conflicts of interest, lack of transparency, and lack of integrity undermine democracy. She also cites research that supports regulated capitalism as the most effective way to ensure long-term economic security that benefits the broad population and not just a few at the top of the income and wealth scales.

There has never been a more urgent time for us to look in the mirror and candidly assess how we are running our country. It is an awesome responsibility we all share. *The Character of American Democracy* provides us insight and guidance on how to do it better.

THE CHARACTER OF AMERICAN DEMOCRACY

—⚒—

INTRODUCTION

Ethics Are Fundamental to Democracy

Character, in the long run, is the decisive factor in the life of an individual and of nations alike.

PRESIDENT THEODORE ROOSEVELT[1]

YEARS BACK, WHILE SERVING AS a member of the US House of Representatives, I was walking from the Capitol to my rental apartment one evening when I ran into a very powerful congressional committee chairman. He was standing on the sidewalk in front of a quite nice, and quite expensive, restaurant. After we exchanged greetings, he invited me to join him and other members of Congress for dinner in the restaurant's upstairs private dining room.

That invitation posed a dilemma for me. I personally respected the chairman, and his position meant he could be very helpful to me in serving the interests of the people in my congressional district. But I knew that lobbyists would be paying for the dinner, and I had a personal policy against accepting anything, even a cup of coffee or soft drink, from a lobbyist. Additionally, I had introduced legislation banning members from accepting such gifts. Although the practice is prohibited today, at that time, it was both legal and common for lobbyists to buy meals for members of Congress.

I quickly made the decision to join the chairman and his group, but I only drank a Diet Coke and the next day reimbursed one of the lobbyists who was cohosting the event. During the dinner, the wife of one of my House colleagues asked me why I was not eating. As discreetly as possible, I told her that I didn't accept meals paid for by lobbyists. She appeared puzzled by the response and quite casually replied that she and her husband would never be able to eat in

1

such nice restaurants if they had to pay for their own meals. Overall, it was an awkward situation; I was concerned others might perceive me as ill-mannered or self-righteous.

It was clear to me that none of the other members of Congress at the table that evening thought it was inappropriate for lobbyists to buy them dinner. They apparently saw no conflict of interest. But lobbyists are pragmatic and would not spend money on meals for elected officials if they thought they wouldn't be getting a return on their "investment." To them, buying the meal was a relatively inexpensive way to gain access and influence with lawmakers. That practice of hosting dinners for members of Congress gave lobbyists an unfair advantage over constituents, who did not have similar opportunities to sit and dine with their representatives or senators.

I also opposed those lobbyist-hosted dinners because of my familiarity with a study conducted many years earlier. Researchers at Yale University found that people were more likely to be persuaded about a specific point of view when they were given peanuts and Pepsi-Cola as they read materials promoting it than when they were given no refreshments.[2] If people can be influenced while eating peanuts and drinking Pepsi, they are likely to also be influenced by an expensive meal in a fine restaurant. Anyone who has ever flown coach or economy class knows the airlines believe peanuts and soft drinks make us more agreeable.

Not everyone will be persuaded or "bought" with a single dinner. But when someone is invited to meals on multiple occasions, an expectation and maybe even a feeling of entitlement can develop. The person buying the meal presumes he or she will be rewarded for the effort. Over time, a habit of accepting even inexpensive meals or refreshments can make a public official more willing than otherwise to support the benefactor's positions or demands.

Many of my former colleagues viewed socializing with lobbyists as a way of conducting business, but I saw it as a violation of the democratic principle of equal access in the legislative process.

The very powerful chairman who invited me to attend the dinner that evening was later convicted on corruption charges, and he served time in prison. Upon his death, he was praised by both Democrats and Republicans for his leadership and compassion. He worked hard and was down-to-earth, and I sincerely admired him. To this day, I believe he was a genuinely decent man. But he was human, of course. And like many people, he probably had never taken the time to seriously and diligently reflect on what constitutes ethical behavior. He had simply become accustomed to the trappings of power, and he apparently did not recognize when he crossed a line. He was surrounded by others who viewed their respective positions similarly; any opportunity for such self-reflections would certainly be countered by the existing mores of "go along and get along."

As a leader in Congress, this chairman advocated for the underserved and fought for equity in public policy. He was earnest in his efforts to develop legislation that created opportunity and fairness for the people of our country. Very sadly, however, he failed to understand that in the development of public policy, the process and outcome are both important. In a democratic society, *how* we make deals is as important as the deals we make. We must be forthright and equitable in the creation and adoption of our laws, not just in their content. The ends, no matter how desirable, do not justify means that favor the input of the rich and powerful over the input of the general population. All of us, leaders and citizens alike, have a responsibility to play fairly and equitably in the governing process. And more broadly, we also have a responsibility to play the game of life in an honest, fair, and equitable manner.

Why do I tell this story as an introduction to a book on ethics and American character? Without ethics, democracy cannot survive. I believe that democracy is only as effective as its ability to execute a truly democratic process. It requires fairness, but there is nothing fair about public officials giving priority to those who have money and influence over the very people those public officials have been elected to represent. Democracy works only if those who hold public office recognize they are conducting the people's business—not the rich, connected, and powerful people's business. We must cherish and uphold the rights of the governed.

And we must never forget that public officials work for us. In doing so, they are supposed to represent a cross section of their constituents, and their actions should be reflective of those they serve. Without ethics, a democratic society is doomed to fail. We must elect people who understand the role ethics play in democracy, and we must hold our public officials to high ethical standards.

I decided to write this book because for a very long time, I have been committed to ethics in government. And I have long been concerned that too many of our people, including government and corporate leaders, pay too little attention to the ethical aspects of conducting the people's business. Quite disconcertingly, since beginning work on this project, I have grown even more troubled by a lack of character and ethics among many who hold positions of leadership in both the public and private sectors. It is also troubling that the public outcry has not been more widespread.

I came of age during the Vietnam War and the Watergate scandal, so I am not naive about the deceit perpetrated by some who serve in high office. In my many years of political engagement, however, I do not recall ever witnessing anything as blatant as what I see today. According to the *Washington Post* Fact Checker, in 2018, the president of the United States averaged more than fifteen false or misleading claims a day.[3] Lee Edwards, a distinguished fellow at the Heritage Foundation, has written that dishonesty is nothing new among presidents, pointing out that Lyndon Johnson misled us on the war in Vietnam and Richard Nixon denied involvement in the Watergate burglary.[4]

News outlets regularly cite political leaders in both major parties for being less than upright in their claims. Examples include a prominent democratic senator for assertions he made regarding the costs of a single-payer health care bill he introduced[5] and a democratic US representative for exaggerations and misstatements of basic facts.[6] I think it is important to distinguish between an occasional misstatement and a daily habit of deliberate untruths. Regardless of frequency or motive, when political leaders do not speak the truth, there is a cost to democracy.

The representative cited above defended herself by saying, "I think that there's a lot of people more concerned about being precisely, factually, and semantically correct than about being morally right."[7]

Integrity in public service is important. The issue is not that other presidents or government officials have also been less than honest or that some political positions are more moral than others. Rather, the issue is that dishonesty undermines our democratic process. When political leaders mislead us, it makes it more difficult and time-consuming to find the truth. That makes it more difficult for us to carry forth in our obligations as citizens in a democratic society. And we should all recognize that deliberately misstating facts for political gain is never "morally right."

Like with gifts and patterns of conduct, when political leaders' unseemly deceptions turn into a constant stream, each more outrageous than the previous, we become inured to the conduct. What is inappropriate becomes routinized and begins to look normal. This is not acceptable and should never be construed as the norm.

My worry for our country's future lies not only with those who hold leadership positions, however. It also extends to our citizenry. All of us must stand up and fight dishonesty. When stories of unethical, and even potentially illegal, behaviors are reported by the news media, not enough people acknowledge the problem. Yes, there are some who become involved and take actions to stop the deceitfulness, but far too many of our citizens appear oblivious to the gravity of the misdeeds. They seem to accept the aberrant behavior as normal.

I am also concerned about the lack of seriousness given to the right and responsibility of political participation. Many who are eligible to vote do not exercise that right, and many of those who do vote expend only limited effort learning about the issues and the candidates.

For a democratic society to survive and thrive, its leaders and citizenry must understand how unethical behavior threatens democracy's very existence. The relationship between strong ethics and a strong democracy is so basic, but many seem to only vaguely recognize and understand this relationship. Research shows that most people believe they are ethical[8] and that they want their leaders to be ethical. A major challenge we face, however, is that many people have only a foggy notion of what constitutes ethical or unethical conduct.

Our nation is facing an ethical crisis that spans the citizenry to top leadership in government and in business. The impact is felt by all, including the most ethical among us.

I am not alone in my concern for our country's future. According to Gallup, polling in 2018 showed confidence in the presidency to be lower than it was immediately following the Watergate scandal. Additionally, during the years 2009–2018, the public's confidence in Congress has been lower than in any other similar time period in the last forty years. And the number of people who have confidence in big business is also low.[9]

Centuries ago, the Greek philosopher Heraclitus taught his followers that character is destiny. He believed lives are not preordained; rather, what we do impacts what happens to us. Quite simply, character matters. Ethics should be front and center in every decision we make and every action we take, but all too often, that is not the case.

Character and ethics play a very significant role in the success of individuals, communities, and entire societies. All of us regularly face ethical dilemmas, and over time, the choices we make determine the person we ultimately become. The more honorably we behave, the more honorable we become. The better our choices and behavior, the better our lives. When people behave honorably, they make their communities and their countries stronger and better.

This is true not just for individuals but also for governments and private-sector organizations. Research shows that government corruption lowers business investment and, therefore, lowers economic growth.[10] When nations conduct business with honor and integrity, they become more trusted, and this trust leads to greater long-term economic growth and strength.[11] In one study on corruption in state government, it was found that average state-government per-capita spending was higher for more corrupt states than less corrupt states.[12] It was also found that states with higher levels of corruption carry higher debt than other states.[13]

My home state of Indiana faces its own challenges in fighting corruption. In 2018, the Coalition for Integrity assigned Indiana a low ranking on the States with Anti-Corruption Measures for Public officials (SWAMP) Index,[14] and my state earned a D- from the 2015 State Integrity Investigation.[15] I cannot help but wonder if this contributes to Indiana's lower median household income and lower overall child well-being.[16] Other research has also found that unethical business behavior negatively impacts a company's stock value.[17]

The United States has long been a world leader through the joint strengths of democracy, capitalism, and trustworthiness. Having the trust of our people and our allies is a necessary component to sustained strength. When political or corporate expediency takes precedence over truth and honor, we lose the trust of others, whose support is essential to our continued success. Additionally, the quality of our decision-making suffers when our decisions are based on falsehoods rather than on facts. And poor decision-making leads us in a direction that is neither good nor sustainable.

The future of our nation and world depend on the quality of America's character. In writing this book, I am hoping to address what I believe is the heart of this problem: we need greater integrity and stronger character. We won't be our best as a nation and society unless all of us—public officials, corporate leaders, workers, and citizens—make it a priority to uphold the highest of ethical standards. We need to be as dedicated to ethics and character as we are to ourselves and our families. No matter who we are or what we do for a living, we all have an obligation to live ethical and accountable lives. Without ethics and character, we cannot be our best selves or do our best for our families. And neither can we reach our potential as a nation.

Living a good and successful life is not easy, and neither is it easy to build a strong and enduring democracy. But making ethical choices will improve the long-term probability of our success. I would rather live my life in a democracy than in any other form of government, and I want the United States to stay strong.

Unethical leadership is a threat to democracy. Those who serve in high office have an obligation to disclose personal interests that might interfere with their ability to serve the public interest. And the citizenry has the responsibility, as well as the right, to demand such disclosure.

A president of the United States who refuses to make his or her income-tax returns public or to place his or her financial holdings in a blind trust is undermining the democratic principle of equal access to participation in the governing process. We must have a way to keep a check on leaders who might give priority to those who can strengthen their financial position at a cost to the public good. A leader must demonstrate that policy decisions are based on merit and the good of the people, not on one's personal financial interests. This is especially so in a global economy where there must never be any doubt that the president's foreign policy decisions are made in the best interest of our country and not in the best interest of his or her wallet.

When a president meets or talks with a foreign dignitary, there should never be any discussion of his or her financial interests or holdings. There must never be any suggestion that a relationship exists, or could exist, between the official policies of the United States and the financial interests of the person who serves in the Oval Office. And there must never be a connection between the president's financial interests and the official policies he or she advances.

The president of the United States, like every other employee of the federal government, works for us. For democracy to work, our national interests must always take precedence over his financial interests. We have a right to know the full extent of a president's financial interests.

Covered in the book are ethics issues we all face every day, regardless of our religious beliefs, personal values, or line of work. I have attempted to make a strong and practical case for ethical living and leadership. Toward that end, I have included a brief review of the teachings of some of the world's great moral philosophers. Additionally, the book contains real-life challenges that cause us to behave in ways that do not reflect the best in humanity. And I present a pragmatic, analytical approach to strategic ethical decision-making.

This work is not a comprehensive catalogue of the study of ethics and morality. I leave that kind of analytical writing to the philosophers. Rather, it is a personal analysis of what my own experiences and academic work have taught me about human behavior, ethics, and the success of individuals, organizations, and societies. It is my hope that the content will be used in a way that makes us stronger as a nation and society. I have worked to keep the writing as concise and easy to read as possible so that the book can become a practical resource for anyone aspiring to a higher level of ethics and character in business, in government, or in life.

Throughout this book, I reference an array of people and organizations that have demonstrated great character. In doing so, I am not suggesting that they are perfect or that every action they have taken is a model of morality. And I do not hold myself out to be the prototype of ethical perfection; I realize there have been many times when I have made less than perfect choices.

I also know that this country I love is not perfect. We do not always demonstrate the character inspired by the Declaration of Independence and our Constitution, particularly when we discriminate against others. Every time we allow entire groups, or even one person, to be marginalized, we are not upholding the principles embraced by our nation's founders. In the past two and a half centuries, we have struggled, hobbled, and even backstepped. Our overall record, however, is one of forward movement in advancing equity and opportunity for humankind. We still have a long way to go, but I am eternally thankful to be a citizen of the United States of America.

One does not have to be perfect to be a person of character. But living or leading with character does require a serious and continuous effort to seek truth and to make choices that respect the worth of the other people and other beings who inhabit our world. We can do better. And if we do better, we will be better—as individuals, as communities, as a nation, and as a world.

There is much work yet to be done. Even though time and experience show us we are at our best when we act with principle, our citizens and our leaders do not always behave honorably. I think that most of us are trying hard to do the best we can with what we've got. But we should not be satisfied until we are giving it our best effort. Another inspiration for writing this book is my personal belief that we must each do everything we can to be good citizens of our great country. When we work hard to be our best selves, we make America better, and that makes for a better world, but we can be our best only if we understand the central role of ethics.

It is my belief that ethics are critical to a democratic society's long-term, sustained success, and it is my objective to make a convincing case for that in this book.

ONE

—ᴍ—

AMERICAN CHARACTER

A people that values its privileges above its principles soon loses both.

PRESIDENT DWIGHT D. EISENHOWER[1]

LIKE MANY CHILDREN ACROSS THE United States growing up in the 1950s and 1960s, I was privileged to be part of a neighborhood filled with military veterans. These men and women were the foundation of our community. They and their families believed in and were committed to the greater good of society. Everywhere I went in those days—to our church, to the 4-H fair, to the feed mill, to the grocery store—there were always veterans of World War II or the Korean War present. Many of our neighbors, as well as my own dad and uncles, had been deployed to foreign countries during their military service, and they would often talk about their experiences and travels. My late mother-in-law, who grew up on a family farm in rural northern Indiana, volunteered to serve in the US Army Air Forces and was deployed to serve in England. As a young woman in civilian life, she was known for her strength and resolve. But as with her fellow soldiers, her interminable mettle and allegiance were fully revealed during her military service.

As a child, I gave little thought to how much had been asked of those veterans and their families. I also gave little thought to their bravery. Most of the veterans I knew lived on grain and livestock farms, and they were very tied to their land and their communities. They worked seven days a week, and they rarely traveled outside our home state of Indiana. As children, many of them had barely journeyed to a neighboring county, and most of them rarely, if ever, traveled to large cities. One could imagine they all would have found it at least

9

a little daunting to travel across country. And yet, as young men and women, some of them just teenagers, they answered the call to travel anywhere in the world and risk their lives in defense of our country and our democratic values. They lived and breathed patriotism and courage.

In his book *The Greatest Generation,* Tom Brokaw wrote the following about the men and women who served during World War II, "At a time in their lives when their days and nights should have been filled with innocent adventure, love, and the lessons of the workaday world, they were fighting, often hand to hand, in the most primitive conditions possible, across the bloodied landscape of France, Belgium, Italy, Austria. They fought their way up a necklace of South Pacific islands few had ever heard of before and made them a fixed part of American history—islands with names like Iwo Jima, Guadalcanal, Okinawa. . . . They stayed true to their values of personal responsibility, duty, honor, and faith."[2]

More than sixteen million men and women from farms, towns, and cities across the country served in our US military during World War II.[3] In the last two and a half centuries since the American Revolution, tens of millions of service members have protected and continue to protect our democratic principles and our people. The embodiment of selfless courage and patriotism, they are men and women of American character.

At its very core, democracy demands courage and strength, and service members and veterans are the incarnation of great courage and strength. They reflect the character imagined by our nation's founding fathers and are the embodiment of selfless courage and patriotism. They are men and women of American character.

THE MEANING OF CHARACTER

Before we can understand how to incorporate character into our decision-making or our leadership, we must first recognize what it is. The term is derived from the Greek word *charaktêr* and was originally used to denote a marking or an imprint on a coin.[4] Coins, of course, are a form of currency, and different markings reflect different monetary values. Just as a coin's imprint reflects its value in the marketplace, a person's imprint on society determines the value he or she adds to or subtracts from our world.

Character can be positive, negative, or even neutral. Aristotle held a belief in excellences of character, meaning the "combination of qualities that make an individual ethically admirable." His phrase for excellences of character— *êthikai aretai*—is usually translated as moral virtues or moral excellence(s). The

Greek *êthikos* is the adjective cognate with *êthos*, or *character*. In other words, according to Aristotle, a person of character is one who demonstrates moral virtue in his or her actions.

Although one's character could be either honorable, corrupt, or somewhere in between, the term is often used to mean something positive, as reflected in the statement "She is a woman of character." Unless otherwise indicated, that is how the word is used throughout this book.

What is American character? I believe the answer to this question lies in the values set forth in our nation's founding documents, the Declaration of Independence and the Constitution. In officially declaring our independence from England, the forefathers established the fundamentals of our nation's character when they wrote,

> We hold these Truths to be self-evident, that all Men are created equal, that they are endowed by their Creator with certain unalienable Rights, that among these are Life, Liberty, and the Pursuit of Happiness—That to secure these Rights, Governments are instituted among Men, deriving their just Powers from the Consent of the Governed, that whenever any Form of Government becomes destructive of these Ends, it is the Right of the People to alter or to abolish it, and to institute new Government, laying its Foundation on such Principles and organizing its Powers in such Form, as to them shall seem most likely to effect their Safety and Happiness.

As a living document, the Constitution is both aspirational and inspirational, but it also provides very constructive and pragmatic parameters for fair and equitable self-governance. The Constitution of the United States of America reflects the principles of strong character. The fifty-two words of its preamble may be the greatest mission statement ever written: "We the People of the United States, in Order to form a more perfect Union, establish Justice, insure domestic Tranquility, provide for the common defence, promote the general Welfare, and secure the Blessings of Liberty to ourselves and our Posterity, do ordain and establish this Constitution for the United States of America."

These historic documents created the foundation for a fair and open democratic government that values individuals and individual rights. They established the principles that are integral to our nation's character. They are great and illustrious documents. But as inspiring and impressive as these documents are, they are not perfectly written. The Declaration of Independence would have more character if it stated that "all people" rather than merely "all men" are created equal. The US Constitution has been amended numerous times. It took until 1870 for the nation to ratify the Fifteenth Amendment prohibiting denial of voting rights based on race, and the Nineteenth Amendment prohibiting the denial of voting rights to women was not ratified until 1920.

Democracy places great value on individual rights, freedoms, and justice. And at its very core, democracy is an ethical concept and an ethical way to govern because it is "a system of government in which effective political power is vested in the people."[6] As we know, the first democratic government was created in Athens, and the word *democracy* comes from the terms *demos*, meaning the people, and *kratos*, meaning power. In other words, democracy means "capacity to do things" or "power of the people."[7] Not only is democracy a fair way to govern; it also provides the potential for the building of a stronger society. British philosopher John Stuart Mill argued that giving political power to the masses requires those in decision-making or leadership positions to consider the varied interests of all, which leads to more balanced policy-making. He argued further that broadening sources of information improves the quality of decision-making.[8] I believe the broad-based discussions integral to the democratic process improve critical assessment and moral awareness. While democracy itself is an ethical concept, its very design can enhance the character of a people.

Other forms of government do not place the same value on equity or on a person's rights and liberties. For example, in a totalitarian government, a small group of elites controls the political, economic, and even social and cultural activities of a society. With no respect for the citizenry, the leadership uses various means to control their behavior. In a dictatorship, a single person controls virtually everything and has no accountability to the general population. There is also singular control in an absolute monarchy, where bloodlines determine who will be king or queen. Socialism appears to be well-intentioned, with its commitment to sharing of assets, but it ignores the rights of the individual to make personal economic decisions. And communism, which Karl Marx argued would cure the ills of inequality in a society, is also a form of government that disregards the rights of individuals to have and follow their own will.[9]

Merging democracy and capitalism, as we have done in the United States, has created what is widely recognized as a uniquely powerful force. Not as widely recognized, however, are the strong ethical principles embodied in this combination. While democracy is lauded by many, capitalism is regularly maligned as favoring the rich and mighty. Capitalist economies have been more successful at growing markets and wealth than other economic structures, and it has long been my belief that a market-based economy provides the greatest potential for economic opportunity.[10]

I also believe that the key to a market economy that best serves society in the long run is well-thought-out public policies that include effective regulation. No economic system works perfectly, and in every type of structure, there are ebbs and flows in opportunity and growth. But in a capitalist structure, the cause of economic disadvantage lies not as much with the type of economy as with the people who take advantage of, or even abuse, their position within it. A smartly designed regulatory system provides needed balance.

Capitalism "is a system where the means of production are owned privately and operated for profit. It is a system opened to new ideas, new firms and new owners where decisions on investment, production, trade and pricing are largely determined by market forces. This does not mean that the state has no role in capitalism. On the contrary, the state needs to create the appropriate regulatory and legal framework without which markets will not function properly. Also, the state needs to provide public goods and ensure that there is adequate physical and human infrastructure."[11] Opportunity creation through the private right to property and commerce is a virtuous concept that exemplifies respect for the individual and the right of personal ownership. The incentives for economic growth that this structure provides also offer potential for a better quality of life for individuals, families, and entire communities.

This is not to suggest that capitalism is perfect. Private ownership of property and freedom to choose what to buy or sell are not the only components of capitalism. Self-interest is also central to capitalism. As Adam Smith wrote in *The Wealth of Nations*, "It is not from the benevolence of the butcher, the brewer, or the baker that we expect our dinner, but from their regard to their own interest."[12] The business owner wants to make a profit from the sale of goods, but the customer also acts in his or her own rational self-interest, which means that both the buyer and seller must address each other's wants. In a market economy, there is power on both sides of the transaction.

A major challenge facing market economies is ensuring balance and equity. Research has shown that income inequality negatively affects economic growth and sustainability. While there is not a one-size-fits-all formula, an International Monetary Fund working paper makes a strong case for public policy that mitigates the challenges of income inequality. Specifically, "when the rich get richer, benefits do not trickle down," but policies that promote development of human capital and progressive tax systems are effective in advancing income equality.[13]

I believe that the combination of self-governance, personal ownership, and private business enterprise provides the best opportunity for individuals and societies to flourish and endure. The challenge in making this combination work is ensuring that the operationalization or implementation of the principles embraced by democracy and capitalism are protected by a government that is fairly and equitably run by the governed. Ethics and laws are essential. Upholding, protecting, and nurturing individual and societal interests require an informed, engaged, and ethical citizenry, as well as ethical leadership in government and business. Not only do we all have a role to play in this system, but we all have a responsibility to be honest, informed, and engaged.

As a democratic republic with a capitalist economy, the United States of America has always had a principled mission. We have not perfectly executed our mission, because as a nation of humans, we are imperfect. Humans tend to act in ways they believe will best serve their own self-interest, and doing so often conflicts with society's interests. Additionally, rarely do we have perfect knowledge, so we often think we are acting in a way that will benefit us when, in fact, we are behaving in a way that is not in our best interest. We are imperfect decision-makers.

Our imperfections make ethics necessary for protecting the values that are integral to our democratic mission. Ethics and laws set parameters that establish a realm of actions we determine to be acceptable. In the government arena, codes of ethics that are enforced help protect our democratic principles, our form of government itself, and our individual rights as persons. They also remind our officials that we are watching them, provide standards by which levels of acceptable conduct may be measured, and offer bright lines of demarcation between what is legal and what is not. Enforcement is also necessary.

Professional ethics and laws do not tell us what our personal morality or religious beliefs should be. Rather, they set standards of behavior that help us protect the principles of democracy and the rights we are guaranteed under the Constitution.

History tells us that many of the original settlers who came here from Europe did not show great character in their treatment of others, and today the struggle to overcome selfishness, unconscious biases, and bigotry continues. But there is no question that the framers of our Constitution had an honorable and enlightened vision for our country. They combined the idealism of the time with the pragmatic mechanics of self-governing. We must never ignore or question the responsibility each of us holds to keep that vision alive—not just for today but also for those who follow behind us.

From our very beginning as a nation, we have not just placed high value on economic security and homeland security, but we have also believed in and aspired to something even greater. Equality and fairness, individual rights and liberties, and the greater good are all valued here. These values have been instrumental to our successes and have made us the world leader we are. Our mission is more than a mere endeavor to do things right; it is also an endeavor *to do the right things.* I believe that to be our best as a society, we must work hard do the right thing in our personal lives as well as in our government and corporate actions. We know that every individual has worth, and we believe that liberty and opportunity are basic human rights. Our deeds must reflect those ideals.

The founding fathers made these values a priority. When they wrote our Constitution, they placed a strong focus on the rights of the individual in the governing process. Their goal was to create a nation that values equality, transparency, and opportunity. Democracy is so much more than a form of government; it is an embodiment of virtuous principles and ethical ideology.

The way we and our leaders enact policy matters as much as the policy that is enacted. There are always consequences to what we do and how we do it. When elected officials "misbehave," the public becomes frustrated and loses faith and trust in the democratic process. But we must always remember that as much as the character of our leaders matters, so does the character of our citizens. Every one of us has the responsibility to be informed and honest in conducting our own affairs, in carrying out our work responsibilities, and in choosing our elected leaders. I believe that the integrity of our elected officials is a direct reflection of the integrity of our citizens.

A strong United States of America is important to the well-being and security of the world, not just to the best interest of those who live here. Our country is an amazing experiment in democracy and capitalism. What we do and how we do it have significance around the globe. We must remind ourselves every day that our businesses, our governments, and, most importantly, our people can be a model for a stronger, safer, fairer, and better world. Anything less fails to uphold the vision our founding fathers had for our nation.

Building and maintaining character are critical to our future. It is not possible to do so, however, unless there is a shared understanding of what it means to have character. Our Constitution makes clear the values and principles integral to American character, and we share them as a people of this nation. But values and principles do not stop at our borders. Research findings tell us that around the world, people of different countries, cultures, and religions share what might appropriately be called *universal values.* In other words, the human race—more than seven billion people spread over 197 million square miles of the earth—has a degree of commonality and agreement when it comes to values and character.

PILLARS OF CHARACTER

The Josephson Institute of Ethics identifies six pillars of character that are widely accepted within and across cultures and around the globe: trustworthiness, respect, responsibility, fairness, caring, and citizenship.[14]

One would be hard-pressed to argue against these pillars. Stated slightly differently, we would expect a person of character to be honest and loyal, to treat others as we would like to be treated, to do what we are supposed to do, to be open-minded and play by the rules, to have compassion and be kind, and to be good citizens who add to the value of our community, country, and world. These obligations seem intuitive. Yet, every day, we witness decisions and actions that violate these universal principles.

I believe it requires courage to consistently behave in ways that reflect trustworthiness, respect and caring for others, personal responsibility, fairness of intent and outcome, and good citizenship. I also believe that courage is not intuitive but is developed, and the more we make the effort to behave with courage, the more courageous we become.

Because we are a nation of humans, we are not a perfect country. It is fair to say that there always has been, and continues to be, more unethical behavior than we would like. Bad conduct always harms who we are individually and as a society. Even with our imperfections, however, the United States has a strong history of ultimately doing the right thing. In the following, I present examples of behaviors that lack character and other examples of behaviors that reflect character. In reviewing them, I think it is easy to see how our country has been weakened by bad conduct but strengthened by good conduct.

Trustworthiness

Top executives at Wells Fargo set unrealistic sales goals for the marketing staff, and in attempting to meet these goals, employees created millions of unauthorized customer accounts. In doing so, they demonstrated that the bank was not trustworthy. Not only have their employees and customers been damaged by these actions; the bank itself paid a price in lost revenues, volatility in share value, and lawsuit settlements.[15]

Captain Chesley Sullenberger, an Air Force Academy graduate and a now-retired airline captain, has been widely recognized for his great courage and skill. He demonstrated both when he executed a successful landing on the Hudson River, after a bird strike destroyed both engines of his US Airways Airbus A320 aircraft. His actions epitomize a man worthy of great trust.

The preparation needed to accomplish the landing required the highest levels of seriousness, hard work, and discipline, all aimed at ensuring that airline passengers could trust the captain to successfully confront the most unexpected and challenging of circumstances. After landing the plane and helping evacuate all the passengers, he twice walked the aisle, to and from the rear of his airplane, to ensure that there was no one left on board. Captain Sullenberger personifies trustworthiness.

Yet, as anyone who watched the Tom Hanks cinematic portrayal knows, he was subjected to considerable second-guessing and was made to account for his actions. In the end, his reputation remained intact. But his experience, as well as the experience of the investigators, illustrate the many dilemmas faced in ethical decision-making.

Respect

Historically, our country has not always shown great respect for women and minorities. Section 1 of the Fourteenth Amendment to the Constitution, ratified in 1868, guarantees women full rights of citizenship, but Section 2 of the same amendment defines "citizens" and "voters" as "male." And many states continued to pass and uphold laws that allowed discrimination against women. Additionally, many schools allowed discriminatory practices until the passage of Title IX of the Education Amendments, which prohibits gender discrimination by any educational institution receiving federal financial assistance. Even after the Fifteenth Amendment prohibiting denial of the right to vote "on account of race, color, or previous condition of servitude" was ratified in 1870, many state and local governments created barriers to make it difficult for minorities to vote. It took almost a century before these practices were prohibited by the Voting Rights Act of 1965.

President George H. W. Bush and Congress showed long-overdue respect when they supported the Americans with Disabilities Act (ADA). Senator Tom Harkin of Iowa was chief sponsor of the bill that became law in 1990. The ADA was widely recognized as the most comprehensive civil rights legislation since the 1964 Civil Rights Act. Today, one might wonder why it took so long to statutorily protect these rights. But at the time, there was strong opposition by some powerful forces, including the National Federation of Independent Business.[16] President Bush, Senator Harkin, and many others understood that disabilities do not stop people from making all kinds of contributions that strengthen our nation and world. Adopting this legislation was a demonstration of respect for millions of individuals and the contributions they make to a stronger America.

It also demonstrated respect for the truth that opportunity makes it possible for all of us to make a positive impact.

Responsibility

Elected officials who support fiscal policies that result in unsustainable deficit and debt levels are being irresponsible. Government debt, like private debt, is the result of spending levels that exceed revenue levels. While public debt is not inherently bad and can even provide net positive benefits to a community, a state, or the country, the level must be sustainable. Sustainability is partly determined by the size and health of the private sector economy. Whether Democrat, Republican, or other, and whether serving at the local, state, or federal level, public officials have an obligation to make fiscally responsible decisions. It is their duty to the taxpayers who have elected them and, maybe even more, to the children who will be forced to carry the debt burden in the future.

US Senator Tammy Duckworth is widely recognized for her courage; throughout her life, she has also demonstrated a deep sense of personal responsibility to her fellow citizens and her country. As a Blackhawk helicopter pilot in the Illinois Army National Guard, she was one of the first women to fly combat missions in Operation Iraqi Freedom. Her helicopter was struck by a rocket-propelled grenade. The attack cost her both legs and the partial use of one of her arms, but it did not stop her from continuing in public service. Prior to her election to the Senate, she led the Illinois Department of Veterans Affairs, was appointed by President Obama to serve as an assistant secretary at the US Department of Veterans Affairs, and was also elected to serve in the US House of Representatives.[17] When asked about the war in Iraq and her mission's worthiness, she responded, "I was hurt in service for my country. I was proud to go. It was my duty as a soldier to go. And I would go tomorrow."[18] Her words and actions epitomize personal responsibility.

Fairness

In violation of federal regulations, a former assistant secretary of telecommunications and information at the Department of Commerce hosted a dinner party at her home that was paid for by companies she was responsible for regulating.[19] In addition to being illegal, this party also violated the principle of fairness in the democratic process. In her role as a regulator, she had the power to impact entities regulated by her agency. Those companies, therefore, would likely believe that if they did not comply with her request to underwrite the social event, she could create problems for them in the future. It is unfair to these companies to ask them to underwrite the party. Additionally, the former assistant secretary may view these same companies more favorably because of their financial support of her party, resulting in more advantageous treatment by her in the future. That would be unfair to other companies who did not help pay for the event. Fairness in a democratic society demands a clear separation between a public official's personal interests and the rights and interests of the public. A government employee must not accept something of value from persons or entities who have interests that can be impacted by the decisions that employee makes in his or her official capacity.

Starbucks sets a strong example of fairness with the compensation and benefits packages it offers employees. Benefits include life insurance, health and dental coverage, 100 percent tuition for undergraduate study through Arizona State University's online programs, a contribution match for their 401(k) program, and a discounted stock purchase plan.[20] These benefits exceed what is typical in the food and beverage service industry.

Caring

As consumers, when we knowingly choose products manufactured by children working in unsafe sweatshops, we are not demonstrating that we care about them. According to estimates based on data collected by UNICEF, the International Labour Office, and the World Bank, approximately 168 million children around the world are engaged in the paid and unpaid workforce. For more than half of them, the work compromises their health and safety, and/or their moral development.[21] There is no quick or simple answer to this problem, as many families are dependent on the meager wages these children earn. We have the obligation, however, to care enough to be informed and to take actions toward eliminating the practice.

After the late W. K. Kellogg and his brother inadvertently flaked wheat berry, he continued experimenting until he created the corn flake. In 1906, he founded what is known today as the Kellogg Company. During the Great Depression, out of concern for the many who were desperate for employment, he made the decision to split shifts so that he could hire new employees.[22] At the same time, he also established the W. K. Kellogg Foundation for the purpose of "administering funds for the promotion of the welfare, comfort, health, education, feeding, clothing, sheltering and safeguarding of children and youth, directly or indirectly, without regard to sex, race, creed or nationality." He gifted equity shares to the foundation to ensure that it would live on, as it does today, supporting programs in the United States and beyond.[23] His philanthropic acts demonstrate great care for others.

Citizenship

We should all strive to do what is in the best interest of our communities, our country, and our world. It is important that we put forth effort to be informed and engaged as well as to recognize the ways that our own behavior can have a positive or negative impact. When we make a habit of getting our news from biased outlets that confirm what we already believe or what we want to believe, whether the news source tilts to the left or to the right, we are not taking citizenship as seriously as we should.

It does not matter if we are a member of the Democratic Party or the Republican Party or if we are independent. To be good citizens, we should seek the truth, not the confirmation of our political leanings and personal biases. One can only imagine how different and more civil political dialogue might be if regular viewers of conservative news programs were to spend an hour or two each week tuned in to progressive news programs and did so with an open mind, while those who regularly watch progressive programs were to view conservative programs.

WHAT IT MEANS TO ACT ETHICALLY

US congressman John Lewis of Georgia exemplifies citizenship at the highest level. Born in 1940, the son of sharecroppers, he has lived a life of courageous public service. As a college student and young man, he was a leader in the civil rights movement, risking his own life to lead marches and lunch counter sit-ins.[24] A genuinely modest gentleman, he is a true legend in his own time, having received numerous awards, including the Presidential Medal of Freedom.

Even as these pillars are broadly valued, people quite regularly disregard them. Yet most of us believe we are moral individuals, and we think morality is important. What explains this discrepancy between our beliefs and our behavior?

It may be partly due to a lack of clarity regarding what constitutes righteousness and virtue. I grew up in a small country church that taught us a very narrow definition of morality. We were told it was immoral to tell an untruth, to disobey our parents, to drink alcoholic beverages, or to smoke cigarettes. In one sermon at an evening revival service, a visiting minister condemned the wearing of makeup, calling it an immoral act.

As an undergraduate student at a Christian university, I learned a much-broader definition of morality that included integrity, compassion, personal responsibility, and respect for others. There is no single or simple definition of morality, but the following two definitions from the *Stanford Encyclopedia of Philosophy* help provide clarity. Descriptive morality is the "code of conduct put forward by a society or group (such as a religion), or accepted by an individual for her own behavior," and normative morality is a "code of conduct that, given specified conditions, would be put forward by all rational persons."[25]

These definitions are broad, but both suggest that morality is based on thoughtful analysis and shared values. I have come to believe that integrity is the essence of morality. To act with integrity means to make the effort to seek truth, which requires commitment and, in many cases, critical thinking. When we are honest and deliberate in our actions, we are more likely to recognize the true impact of our behavior, in both the short run and long run. That increases the probability that we will hold ourselves accountable and act in ways that are not harmful to our fellow beings and the world.

Findings from numerous studies in the field of social psychology provide further insight into why most people think they are moral even though their behavior is often unprincipled. The majority of people do not have well-developed moral compasses. As an illustration, many hotels use anti-theft clothes hangers in the guest rooms. The act of stealing clothes hangers from hotel rooms may seem insignificant to the person who is doing so, but it clearly demonstrates lack of trustworthiness and disrespect for another entity's property.

Another challenge we face is the influence that even small gestures can have on our perceptions and judgment. As an example, who would believe they could be more easily influenced if someone bought them dinner? Many of my former colleagues in Congress who were sincere and dedicated public servants simply did not believe that the wining and dining by lobbyists could influence them. But research shows that even small acts of kindness and generosity can influence our behavior; that is why we need legal parameters that minimize the potential for unfair advantage in policy-making.

To reach our potential as a nation, we must move forward together and act with character. This requires a common understanding of what it means to have character and an appreciation of the value of integrity and truth. Additionally, we must also understand the relationship between integrity and long-term,

sustained success. We all need to learn how we can identify the kinds of circumstances and psychological factors that interfere with our ability to make
good choices and do the right thing. Then we must learn how to overcome
these obstacles to ethical behavior. Finally, we must be able to recognize the
difference between personal morality and professional ethics, as well as the
way we can objectively and strategically make principled decisions that lead
to honorable behavior.

Understanding these concepts and influences helps us build a "good behavior" compass, which helps us build character. When we know what influences
human behavior, we can more honestly and accurately assess what we are doing
and why we are doing it. The more we know about ethics and the more we know
about ourselves, the better equipped we are to make ethical decisions.

There is often confusion about what ethics are. In teaching, I have discovered that students find it easier to understand what ethics are by first becoming
familiar with what they are not. While ethics are important to most religions,
they are not religious beliefs. The rightness or wrongness of a choice or an
action is equally relevant to an atheist or an agnostic as it is to someone who
devoutly obeys specific religious teachings. Ethics are not morals, although
people who are highly moral are also likely to be ethical.

The Greek philosophers defined morality in terms of virtue, and they identified characteristics such as wisdom, courage, self-restraint, and justice as necessary for living a virtuous or moral life. Aristotle believed that virtues lie within
the person but are not always reflected in one's choices or actions.

Ethics are not feelings, even though how we feel about something may provide a signal to us about the appropriateness of an action we are about to take.
A bad feeling will not necessarily lead us down an ethical path. Someone who
finds it thrilling to take chances might feel good about doing something highly
unethical because of the excitement that comes with the risk of being caught. As
a young man, Frank Abagnale Jr., the real-life character featured in the movie
Catch Me If You Can, certainly appeared to find his highly unethical escapades
exhilarating and maybe even enjoyable.

Finally, while it may be unethical to break a law, ethics are not the same as
laws. Many people consider the law to be a standard for behavior, but many
laws, such as those allowing slavery in the early years of our country, are en-
tirely devoid of ethics. Even well-intentioned and well-written laws are, at best,
a minimum ethical standard. A person of character goes beyond simply understanding what the law allows. Just because an action is legal does not mean it
is ethical.

Ethics are based on "well-founded standards of right and wrong that prescribe what humans ought to do, usually in terms of rights, obligations, benefits to society, fairness, or specific virtues."[26] In other words, the intrinsic value of an action combined with the impact the action has on individuals and institutions determine whether a specific behavior is ethical or unethical. Someone who is ethical feels a sense of duty to others and recognizes that virtuous and principled behavior has value.

This definition is comprehensive and pragmatic, and it encompasses both micro- and macroethics. *Microethics* pertain to the decisions and actions of individuals in the context of personal and professional relationships. In business, for example, a microethics issue facing a sales representative would be whether to pad an expense account or to only claim reimbursement for the actual expenses incurred while conducting business. For a government employee, a microethics issue would be to decide if it is appropriate to use government property personally or only for official government business.

Macroethics concern matters of broad or long-term impact. It is not enough for us to just be honest with ourselves on issues of narrow focus; we must also be honest about how our actions will impact the larger society in the long run, as well as in the short run.

In the business sector, the social value of a product and the environmental impact of a manufacturing process are macroethics issues. Government policies generally have a macroethics dimension, because they typically have broad and long-term impact that may or may not be equitable. An example is tax policy and its effect on long-term government debt. Another macroethics issue would be funding levels for the Department of State and the Department of Defense and their subsequent impacts on homeland security.

While microethics have a narrower focus than macroethics, over time microethics decisions can have a macroimpact. As an example, if elected officials behave microethically over time, the public may have more overall confidence in their government. On the other hand, when public officials consistently behave microunethically, people lose faith in government.

It is possible to simultaneously uphold very high microethics standards and very low macroethics standards, or very high macroethics standards and very low microethics standards. For example, a member of Congress could abide by every campaign finance law and every law governing the operation of her congressional office and yet could also deliberately ignore relevant facts when voting on legislation. In doing so, she would support policy that in the long run is not good for the country. She would be microethical and macrounethical. In business, a chief executive officer could be very responsible regarding the company's impact on the environment, but he could inflate his expense account. In such a case, he would be macroethical and microunethical.

MICROETHICS AND PROTECTING DEMOCRACY

Democracy is a form of government whose very design and purpose are macroethical. Its foundation includes universal respect for individuals to self-govern, and it places great value on rights and liberties for all members of society; these are macroethical principles.

One could write volumes about micro- and macroethics. My intent in this book is to show how microethics relate to the broader concept of macroethics. More specifically, violations of microethical principles can undercut the foundational values of democracy as well as the economic principles of capitalism. It is important for those who work in government and business to understand how microethics can positively or negatively impact the broader economy or society.

Our founding fathers recognized both the right and the value of free speech when they wrote the First Amendment to the Constitution, which states, "Congress shall make no law . . . abridging the freedom of speech, or of the press." Open, unencumbered reporting and dialogue are central to democracy. Clearly, if the government controls what we can and cannot say, then we are not free to live our lives as we choose, and we are not allowed to govern as we see fit.

We may not like the way reporters cover a story, or we may disagree with the viewpoints expressed by opinion writers, but in the interest of democracy, we must protect their right to speak. The press is not perfect, but a free press is necessary. When a public official calls a news outlet or a reporter an enemy of the people simply because he or she does not like what is being said, the official is committing an unethical act in the microsense because the statement is self-serving and untrue. Telling an untruth is a violation of ethics at the microlevel.

But this specific action has negative macroconsequences for our country. As a basic requisite of democracy, the free press is not an enemy of the people; it is part of the democratic infrastructure. When an elected official engages in dishonest and self-serving behavior that undermines the free press, his or her actions destabilize the infrastructure of democracy.

On the other hand, reporters and editorial writers who deliberately misrepresent the facts pertaining to the works and leadership of our government are also committing microethics violations that can have macroconsequences. Disseminating falsehoods interferes with the public's ability to access accurate information necessary for effectively participating in the democratic process. Those who deliver the news have a responsibility to deliver the truth.

The public's and the news media's understanding of the role of a free and honest press are both vital to good government. Public officials and the news media must be held to a high standard. This creates a need for professional ethics that establish specific and sometimes narrow parameters for professional behavior. These parameters help ensure that the mission of a government or organization is not undercut by competing interests of various stakeholders.

The Society of Professional Journalists has adopted a strong code of ethics relevant to their work and pertinent to the democratic process. The preamble makes clear the role a free press plays in democracy: "Members of the Society of Professional Journalists believe that public enlightenment is the forerunner of justice and the foundation of democracy. Ethical journalism strives to ensure the free exchange of information that is accurate, fair and thorough. An ethical journalist acts with integrity."[27]

Their code also states that journalists must seek the truth and report it, minimize harm, act independently, and be accountable and transparent. The society recognizes their role as watchdogs over public affairs and the government, and they work to advance transparency in the governing process. The profession has established parameters that include numerous restrictions, including the following: they do not pay sources for information, avoid conflicts of interest, and do not accept gifts or favors that could interfere with their objectivity in reporting the news.[28]

As with any professional group, there are journalists who violate these principles and subsequently undermine the trust that is important for a free press to be its most effective in strengthening the democratic process. But there are many hardworking journalists who spend every day researching and reporting stories that are important to our democracy. We the people also have a responsibility to use discernment in choosing sources of information that have proven credibility.

Micro- and macroethics are both important to a strong society, and we should all strive to be ethical at both levels. Earth is home to billions of fellow humans, not to mention trillions of other animals and plants. No one individual or being owns our planet, and that means we have a responsibility to share everything that is here. Because our actions almost always impact others, we have the obligation to live lives of ethical awareness and to be as disciplined as we can while doing so. To live an ethical life, we must recognize and value the vastness of our world and the importance of all who share it.

A commitment to ethics requires a shared understanding of the parameters, or outer limits, of personal and professional actions. For example, most families have rules regarding how family members are expected to behave and what kinds of choices are considered acceptable. And most formal organizations develop codes of ethics that establish standards of behavior for all who are a part of the organization. The purpose of these rules and policies is to ensure some level of fairness, balance, judgment, and consistency in behavior. They are a way of protecting the rights and interests of others who can be impacted by our individual actions.

Understanding ethics allows people with different religious and moral beliefs to come to agreement about behaviors that are acceptable and respectful of others' rights and interests. Ethics provide protections for individuals, institutions, and the greater good.

CHARACTER GIVES US STRENGTH

We didn't become the most powerful nation in the world because we are smarter than people in other countries. There are smart people everywhere. And we didn't become the most powerful nation in the world because we have more natural resources than other countries. There are natural resources around the globe. Our power comes from a uniquely strong foundation built on democracy, capitalism, and the diversity that comes from immigration. These attributes helped build American character and strength. A participatory government and a private sector economy provide incentives for people to work hard to succeed, while a diverse population inspires creativity and gives us compassion and understanding of others whose experiences are different from our own.

When identifying the qualities that keep us safe and strong, we often overlook the significance of character. We regularly talk about the value of liberty and democratic principles. Over the generations, we have recognized the importance of education, including effective teaching and scholarly research, in creating new opportunities. We have long advanced market expansion and access to capital for growing and strengthening our economy. And we recognize how critical national defense is to our survival.

We also place value on openness and equity in self-governance, and we recognize that the process of governing is as important as the outcome. But sometimes we forget that ethics and character play a very significant role in keeping us strong. In the United States of America, it is not enough to merely adopt effective public policy; there must also be fairness and equity in the way we make our laws.

The First Amendment to the Constitution guarantees the right of free speech, including a free and independent press. We see freedom of expression as a basic human right, and we also believe that it is essential to the democratic process. In a government of, by, and for the people, we must be able to voice our concerns and peacefully assemble. And we recognize that only with a free and independent press will we be able to gather and disseminate the information that is critical to good decision-making by our citizens.

The US Congress was created to be the voice of the people. We are a nation that stands for a fair and open electoral process in which our citizens are guaranteed the right to participate and to vote. The US House of Representatives is often referred to as the "People's House." According to Article I, Section 2 in the Constitution, no one can be appointed to a seat in the House; when a vacancy occurs in the middle of a term, a special election must be called to fill the seat.

Our founding fathers also set constitutionally mandated standards of official conduct for federal officials. In conducting the people's business, Congress is required to do so with transparency. Article I, Section 5 requires both the US House and US Senate to keep and publish a journal of their proceedings.

Article I, Section 9, Clause 8 states, "no Person holding any Office of Profit or Trust under them, shall, without the Consent of the Congress, accept any present, Emolument, Office, or Title, of any kind whatever, from any King, Prince, or foreign State." Receiving something of value from a foreign government could influence a public official to act in that country's interest, rather than in our nation's best interest.

These constitutional requirements are central to our democracy, and we need to keep reminding ourselves that process and outcome are both important to the democratic process.

I was first introduced to politics in 1958, when I was six years old. My father was a Democratic precinct committeeman in rural Whitley County, Indiana, and one of his responsibilities was to identify and register Democratic voters who were new to our community. He and my mother were dairy farmers, and that posed a challenge for them, since evening chores happened to conflict with the best time of day for finding people at home. My mother very graciously volunteered my seven-year-old brother to help Dad with the milking, and she drafted me to be her assistant while she went door-to-door registering new voters.

At each house, she would knock on the door and politely introduce herself. Since she was a Democratic volunteer, she would only register other Democrats. But she was always genuinely friendly and respectful to those who identified themselves as Republicans or independents. If they asked, she would provide them with information on how to register to vote, and she did her best to make them feel welcome in their new neighborhood.

For me, the experience was as much a lesson in citizenship as it was in the political process. By reaching out to our new neighbors and helping register them to vote, my mother was also strengthening the social fabric in our community. Regardless of political affiliation and personal beliefs, we all lived together in the same neighborhood, and we shared common aspirations.

There is strength in numbers, and when the people within a community work together toward a common goal, they accomplish more than when there is division and antagonism. It is also true that communities accomplish more when they work together with neighboring communities rather than when they battle each other as if they are competitors or enemies. From that experience, I developed a belief at a very early age that working together and finding common ground will lead us to a better position than believing "my way is the only way" to solve a problem.

Just as a rising tide lifts all boats, a stronger community benefits all of us who are a part of it. It is better for us to work with our neighbors than to fight with them. And we are better off when our neighbors are doing well than when they are not doing well. If they have the resources to maintain their homes, the value of our own homes will increase. When they pay taxes, those revenues support the local schools, roads, and broader infrastructure that benefit us all.

On a larger scale, good relationships with neighboring countries can be helpful to the United States. We are better off when we have mutually beneficial relationships with other nations than when we have adversarial relationships with them. And if ally countries have strong economies, their citizens will more likely have the purchasing power to buy the products we make, which is good for our own economy. Making allies is better than making enemies.

As a democratic republic with a capitalistic economy, we can be a friend and model for other nations in ways that make us stronger while simultaneously making the world safer and stronger. We have a purpose that is bigger than any individual government and that extends beyond our borders. I believe that our founding fathers clarified this purpose when they wrote the Bill of Rights to establish the limits of government relative to the fundamental rights of the individual.

Their wisdom and foresight were instrumental to us developing into the global leader we have become. At least since World War II, people around the world have frequently turned to the United States as a model when they have addressed issues of international significance. I believe this position we hold is the result of our strength of character, as well as our economic and military might.

In his first inaugural address, Franklin D. Roosevelt so eloquently expressed the importance of working with other nations. When he took office in 1933, our country was in the middle of the Great Depression, and most of his speech focused on domestic policy for addressing the country's huge economic challenges. But he made it clear that he was not advocating for narrow nationalism: "In the field of world policy I would dedicate this Nation to the policy of the good neighbor—the neighbor who resolutely respects himself and, because he does so, respects the rights of others—the neighbor who respects his obligations and respects the sanctity of his agreements in and with a world of neighbors."[29] These words reflect an understanding of the role of the United States in the world; it reflects a belief that we have responsibilities that extend beyond our own borders. They are powerful words.

Many of us believe that President Franklin D. Roosevelt should have engaged our nation earlier and should have been more proactive in fighting the Nazis and in providing refuge to Jews escaping the Holocaust. I think we could have done more had we engaged earlier. Even so, I do not doubt that he understood our nation's role as a player on the world stage, and he recognized that we must not ignore the value of international relationships.

When he first took office, President Roosevelt had to address the very serious economic challenges facing our nation. It has been estimated that 25 percent of our workforce was unemployed in 1933.[30] He took many actions to address these economic issues, including working with Congress and signing the Reciprocal Trade Agreement Act (RTAA) in 1934. By 1939, we had entered into nineteen new trade agreements with other countries. Indeed, "the RTAA served as an integral step in America's transition from economic crisis to global leadership. FDR believed that a complete and permanent recovery depended on strengthened international trade to increase domestic growth and demand. To secure our country's space in the global economy, the American President and Congress needed to work together to negotiate trade agreements to cut tariffs on goods and increase U.S. exports."[31]

He certainly knew that we couldn't be much of a force until we addressed our own economic issues. Hindsight is twenty-twenty, and it is usually easier to second-guess someone else's decisions than to make our own decisions. It is important that our leaders have a sound strategy as well as honorable intent. The strategy President Roosevelt chose may have been the best option given the economic challenges we faced at the time. And we must not forget that he issued an executive order in 1941 that opened national defense and other government jobs to all Americans regardless of race, creed, color, or national origin.[32]

Whatever the reasons for his specific policy decisions in the early years of his presidency, the words of his inaugural address reflect character of leadership that commands global respect. Leadership requires engagement. As in sports, you can't win the championship if you are not on the field, on the court, or in the arena. Those who argue for isolationism ignore the global leadership role of our country. Even more, they do not understand that strategic and smart international engagement makes us stronger. We rarely find effective leadership among those who live the life of a recluse or who are completely self-absorbed. I believe that what is true for the individual is also true for a nation. One can reasonably argue that we not only have principled reasons to engage internationally but we also have practical reasons to do so.

Over the years, there have been many examples of American character and leadership pertaining to our role in the world, but there is no better example than the Marshall Plan. Officially titled the European Recovery Program, the program was conceived by Secretary of State George C. Marshall, who had served as US Army chief of staff during World War II. Through this plan, the United States provided administrative and technical assistance to sixteen European nations whose infrastructures and economies had been torn apart by the war. In total, we provided almost $13 billion (approximately $130 billion, inflation adjusted to 2017) for this effort. The countries' economies recovered, and their rate of growth was unprecedented.[33]

An added benefit of the Marshall Plan was a strengthening of America's relationship with Europe, which led to a new leadership role for the United States on the world stage. In 1953, Marshall, who was known as highly ethical and principled, was awarded the Nobel Peace Prize for his role in developing and implementing the European Recovery Program. Acts of character are often rewarded.

Democracy is an ethical and effective form of government. We should not be surprised to see how the honest practice of democratic principles ensures fairness, improves cost efficiencies, and stimulates economic growth. Nor should we be surprised to know how taking advantage of others and misusing public resources for private gain, also known as corruption, can be very costly. Corruption deters investment and has a negative effect on economic and job growth. It is logical that countries with less corruption "use their human and financial resources more efficiently, attract more investment, and grow more rapidly."[34] And it stands to reason that corruption in state government corre-lates with increased costs of running the government.[35]

Acting with character makes us better leaders. Just as I believe that integrity is the essence of morality, I also believe that it is the essence of character-based leadership. Derived from the same root as *integer*, a whole number, the term *integrity* embodies completeness, balance, and strength. It reflects the values and principles held dear by our founding fathers. In developing our government and writing our Constitution, our nation's founders sought unification, justice, domestic tranquility, security, and liberty for our nation and our people.

Together these concepts and goals are comprehensive, wide-ranging, and inclusive. They embody what it means to have national integrity. They can-not be achieved, however, unless the governing process is truthful. Making a habit of integrity, ensuring that it is a part of everything we do, will build an individual's character, as well as a nation's character.

A person of character recognizes that he or she lives in a world that is shared with others and makes a habit of choosing what is right over merely choosing what he or she wants.

For many people, ethics and character appear to be somewhat elusive. Every day we encounter news stories about political and business leaders, and even everyday citizens, who have behaved badly. Sometimes the behavior is the result of bad intentions, and sometimes it is the result of well-intended but misguided actions. The ethical dilemmas we face can be quite complex, and the right course of action is not always immediately clear. Yet, our lives will be better, more fulfilling, and even easier, if we consistently work to be honest with ourselves and do what is right.

After all is said and done, the value and importance of ethics really should be intuitive. When we lie to ourselves, we make poor decisions, and there is usually a cost. When we lie to others, we lose their trust, and that creates divi-sion. But when we are honest with ourselves, we make better decisions, and the result is to our benefit. When we are honest with others, we earn their trust, and that creates union.

Ethics and character lead us to a more perfect union.

People who are honest with themselves live better lives. Marriages built on trust are better marriages. Businesses whose leaders make decisions based on economic and market realities are more successful. And nations whose public policies are developed from truth are stronger. Philosopher Heraclitus and President Theodore Roosevelt were right. We can live our lives with integrity, or not; we can manage our businesses with integrity, or not; and we can run our governments with integrity, or not. The choices we make will determine our destiny.

If character determines destiny, does that mean you will be successful only if you are ethical? Is it impossible to succeed if you behave unethically? The honest answer to both questions is no. There are many people who regularly take actions that are not ethical but who are still successful. In fact, it would be rare, if not impossible, to find someone whose every decision and every action has been perfectly ethical. But sustained success depends on solid decision-making, which requires candid, factual analysis and truthful, straightforward implementation. Additionally, since most tasks of any significance depend on a team effort, relationships built on trust are essential to getting a job done and moving an organization or society forward.

Obviously, these are good arguments for living a principled life. There are also strong and convincing arguments against living an unprincipled life. Dishonesty is not helpful to the building of relationships necessary for success, and a bad reputation can be costly.

Research shows that the market reacts negatively to corporate scandals.[36] But businesses and governments are not the only entities that are harmed by scandal or fraud. Charitable organizations, for example, are also negatively impacted by disgraceful actions. Scandal and bad publicity may be even more harmful to not-for-profits than they are to businesses.

According to Dr. Stuart Mendel, director of the Center for Nonprofit Policy and Practice at the Maxine Goodman Levin College of Urban Affairs at Cleveland State University, not-for-profits are quite fragile when confronted with bad publicity: "Their whole ability to succeed is based on people's desire to trust them, and they have to appear that they know what they're doing. There is a direct connection of the leadership and the perceived competency of the organization and its ability to raise money. If they didn't handle it right, their fundraising campaigns would be in jeopardy."[37] It has also been found that donations drop when supporters believe executives at a not-for-profit organization are too highly compensated.[38]

We are all very much aware that scandal can ruin one's political career. While not every politician who has misbehaved has been forced from office, recent research clearly shows a negative impact. In fact, a review of the US House of Representatives over a thirty-year period found that less than half of members involved in ethics investigations were reelected to office. Twenty-six percent resigned or retired from office, and 25 percent lost their primary or general election. That contrasts with only 5 percent of those not involved in an ethics investigation losing their primary or general election during that same time period.[39]

What may be even more significant is the impact that scandal appears to have on the public's faith in government institutions. Trust of the federal government has been historically low for some time. In every major national poll in recent years, less than 30 percent of respondents have expressed such trust, and Pew Research found in a March 2019 survey that only 17 percent of Americans expressed trust in Washington to do the right thing. This contrasts with findings in 1964, when 77 percent of respondents said they trusted the federal government.[40]

For a democratic government to be strong, the public needs to have faith and confidence in its leaders and the governing process. This loss of trust in the institution of government is even more significant than the loss of trust in one politician, and elected officials behaving badly can harm all of us. Ethics and transparency are essential to our democratic process.

Our founding fathers understood the fundamental value of character and integrity. Like all of us, they had the imperfections of humanity, and yet they wrote a Constitution of character with the goal of building a nation of character. They placed high value on individual rights and liberties, as well as the responsibilities of citizenship. A democratic form of government that protects freedom of expression provides the setting for disagreement and debate, which can lead to higher aspirations in both the private and public sectors. To realize our potential as a nation in the twenty-first century, we must live every day to uphold the values and character put forth by the founding fathers. And that requires that we communicate with, not yell at, one another.

I think time is of the essence. Effective and strong leadership must be able to address economic and social change in a timely manner. With new technologies, the rate of change in these areas has become more rapid, which means that our nation and world have less time to prepare for and adapt to future challenges. We have a world population of more than seven billion people that is increasing by seventy-five million each year, and that growth creates more environmental, social, economic, and security challenges. The late, world-renowned British physicist Stephen Hawking believed humans could potentially face extinction within the next one hundred to five hundred years, and he identified climate change and artificial intelligence among the challenges that could lead to extinction of the human race.

We don't know if Dr. Hawking's prediction will be proven correct, but we do know that the best way to address serious issues is with integrity and commitment. Without question, there is every reason to move forward with character as expeditiously as we can as we face reality and work together to make our nation and world a better place.

CHALLENGES TO CHARACTER BUILDING

Psychological biases can interfere with our judgment and therefore can affect the choices we make. If we are more persuadable when given a snack of Pepsi and peanuts, as the Yale study indicated, how susceptible are we to being unwittingly influenced? There are a number of studies that provide us with insight. Quite revealing are the findings of research conducted to determine if food can influence whether a medical doctor prescribes a brand name or a generic version of a drug. More specifically, researchers found that physicians who accepted a meal paid for by a pharmaceutical company were more likely to prescribe that company's brand-name drugs than physicians who had not received a meal. The data used for this study were of Medicare subscribers with Part D prescription drug coverage.

The average value of the meals provided to these physicians was less than twenty dollars. Interestingly, this same research also found that doctors who received multiple meals, or meals valued higher than twenty dollars, were even more likely to prescribe the company's brand-name drug.[41]

I think these findings are particularly significant because the practice of medicine is science-based and doctors are known for their objective, technical decision-making. They are highly educated and well trained in using a scientific approach in their profession. If medical doctors can be influenced by the gift of a modest meal, then it would seem likely that most, if not all, of us are persuadable in ways we do not recognize.

There is certainly nothing unethical about prescribing a brand-name drug instead of the generic version of the same drug, if the doctor believes that doing so is in the best interest of the patient. If the decision to prescribe the brand-name drug over the generic version of the drug has been influenced by the gift of a free meal, however, then there is an ethics issue at play. In fact, this specific concern has led many health care providers to prohibit their doctors from accepting such gifts from pharmaceutical companies.

The American Medical Association Code of Ethics contains specific restrictions regarding a physician's acceptance of gifts from entities that have a direct interest in his or her patient treatment recommendations. Doctors may not accept cash from any entity that has a direct interest in the physician's treatment recommendations and may accept an in-kind gift only when it "will directly benefit patients, including patient education" or if the gift is of minimal value.[42] Given the research findings that people were more agreeable after consuming peanuts and Pepsi, one could reasonably argue that doctors should not accept a gift of any value from an entity that has a direct interest in treatment recommendations.

This leads us to another question: if partaking of food and drink makes us gullible, what else might interfere with our good judgment? We may not want to admit it, but it is a fact that our judgment can be manipulated in many ways. And we often make unprincipled decisions based on what we want rather than principled decisions based on what we know is right. There are entire fields of study on behavioral ethics, behavioral economics, and consumer behavior. With all the research in these fields, we are still a long way from having the answers to how our behavior can be manipulated.

Even if we had all the answers, we would continue to be susceptible to influences that interfere with objective, analytical decision-making. I am quite susceptible to all kinds of persuasive techniques even though I hold the PhD in business with a major area of study in marketing and with supporting fields of study in social psychology and statistics.

If medical doctors and marketing professors can be influenced by a modest meal or a clever advertising message, we can only conclude that it is easy to influence decision-making in ways that may not be in the individual's or a society's best interest. Understanding how easily we can be influenced helps us to understand how to counter these tendencies in order to develop ethical behavior and build ethical organizations, including our governments.

THE KEY TO ETHICAL BEHAVIOR AND STRONGER DEMOCRACY

If our judgment can be so easily manipulated, is it even possible for us to consistently make objective and fair decisions? Yes, it is.

The key to ethical behavior is recognizing our human weaknesses and adopting practices that allow us to compensate for them. The more we understand and practice principled decision-making, the more principled we will become. This is true for us individually and for us as a society. Our nation and our democracy are only as strong as the character of our people. This is so for both the citizenry and the leadership. Whether we work in the government, the not-for-profit, or the business sector, all of us must answer the call to uphold the highest of ethical standards.

My decision to write this book is largely the result of a concern about the direction we are headed in and a genuine belief that a strong ethical foundation is essential to democracy's success. The lack of ethics and character among our nation's leaders in both the public and private sectors makes this one of the most disconcerting times in my life. Even more disconcerting is the fact that the public outcry is not as great as it should be. We must fight the tendency among some to see unethical behavior as normal or, even worse, as acceptable.

We the people need to place a greater focus on and develop a better understanding of ethics and character. We should not think of ethics as constraining but as liberating. Living our lives with character creates the potential for us to be our very best selves. What could be more liberating than that? Character is essential to living a productive life, building a strong economy, and running a successful country. The world needs the United States to be strong and to uphold high character.

The freedoms that are integral to our nation should be the global norm, but we will never be able to set the standard for excellence unless we are committed to character-based corporate and government leadership. The more character we have as individuals, the more character we will have as a nation. And only if we are a country of high character will we realize our potential in the decades and centuries to come.

THE CONSTITUTION AND AMERICAN CHARACTER

Recently, a student in one of my ethics classes inquired about a matter pertaining to the Constitution. Not being a lawyer, I was less than fully confident in my ability to correctly and succinctly respond to the question, so I told the class I wanted to verify my answer before addressing the topic. When I pulled a copy of the Constitution from my purse, they all laughed. It is not clear if they were amused because they thought it was nerdy to carry around a copy of the Constitution or if they thought it was old-fashioned to carry a printed copy when an electronic version can be easily accessed on a smartphone. But I carry it in my purse because it serves as a reminder of what we stand for in the United States of America.

In addition to defining our government's structure and authorities, the Constitution sets forth the values and principles that underlie our democracy. Dividing the federal government's authorities among three separate but equal branches ensures balance in the self-governing process. The combination of a discrete and independent judicial system and the requirement that all criminal trials be by jury protects the public from the unfairness that would result from a concentration of power in any one branch of government. And the establishment of a bicameral legislature provides for a more thoughtful and deliberative process than would exist if there were only one legislative body.

The Constitution requires transparency in the legislative process, and it protects our citizens from undue influence by foreign entities with the Emoluments Clause. The Bill of Rights makes clear that the federal government recognizes and gives value to the rights of individuals and the states. We must demand of ourselves and of our leaders strict adherence to the Constitution. It is the document that defines American character, and any violation of its intent is a violation of who we are as a nation.

—๛—

TWO

DECISION-MAKING WITH CHARACTER

Perhaps a man's character was like a tree, and his reputation like its shadow;
the shadow is what we think of it, the tree is the real thing.

PRESIDENT ABRAHAM LINCOLN[1]

SERVING IN THE US HOUSE and in the executive branch were immense
honors for me because of the great privilege of working for my fellow citizens.
I also felt fortunate to work with many public servants who understood the role
of character in good decision-making. There are honorable people serving on
both sides of the aisle.

President George H. W. Bush was someone who demonstrated strong character throughout his life and career. The strength of his statesmanship was very
evident during my first term in the House when he worked with Congress in an
exceptionally nonpartisan way to reach a budget agreement to reduce deficit
spending. His administration and members of Congress met at Andrews Air
Force Base to reach an agreement on the Budget Enforcement Act (BEA) of
1990, which was part of the larger Omnibus Budget Reconciliation Act. The
BEA established discretionary spending caps and pay-as-you-go rules.

As a candidate, he had campaigned on a promise not to raise taxes. But as
the president, he came to believe that there was no economically sound way to
reduce the deficit without targeted tax increases, and he reversed his position
to do what he genuinely believed was in the best interest of the country. This
reversal in position may have cost him his bid for reelection in 1992, but it led
the federal government to a path of deficit reduction.[2] I voted against the Bud-

get Enforcement Act because I believed we needed additional spending cuts beyond those included in the legislation. But I have always admired President Bush for following his own conscience.

President Barack Obama is also a leader of great character, having earned the nickname "No Drama Obama" for his strength and quiet reserve. Both were on display during Operation Neptune Spear, the raid to capture Osama bin Laden, the terrorist mastermind of the attacks on September 11, 2001. As commander in chief, the president listened to both military and civilian advisers; based on their recommendation, he authorized the raid. His top priority was the safety and security of the operators, and he repeatedly made that clear to the Department of Defense. The night before the raid, while the plans were proceeding, he attended the annual White House Correspondents' Dinner, appearing completely composed and relaxed. He gave no indication of the serious operation about to begin. Later, he rightfully gave full credit for taking down the terrorist to the commanders, and especially the Navy SEALs, who exemplify the best of our great military.[3]

Living life with character requires an approach to decision-making that is informed, earnest, straightforward, and deliberate. Leadership with character is built on truth. An ethical leader is someone who gathers the facts before forming an opinion but respects others who hold different opinions. And an ethical leader shows restraint. We know some leaders are highly ethical, while others seem to completely disregard ethics in their decision-making. A primary purpose of professional codes of ethics and laws that set the parameters for acceptable behavior of public officials is to minimize unethical behavior, which undermines democratic principles. By enforcing these standards, we can reduce unethical behavior, even among those leaders who do not have a well-developed moral compass.

CHARACTER AND LEADERSHIP

High character is more than something to be admired. It is also effective. In fact, there is a positive relationship between character-based leadership and an organization's success.

In research on effective corporate leadership, Jim Collins discovered that chief executive officers (CEOs) whose companies were most successful were led by what he called "Level 5" leaders. He conducted empirical research comparing differences between companies that were "good performers" and those that earned cumulative stock returns at least three times that of the general stock market. He found a negative correlation between attention-seeking, celebrity-type leaders and "great" company performance. The leaders of the most successful companies were found to be understated, diligent, and self-effacing.[4]

While he did not specifically measure the CEO's character, he did measure style and approach. He found, for example, that those who were most successful showed respect for colleagues and subordinates. When their companies experienced successes, Level 5 leaders gave the credit to fellow employees, but when they experienced failures, they shouldered the responsibility. Their ambition was for their company's success rather than their personal success.[5] They demonstrated personal responsibility and respect for others, two very important attributes of character.

How does one become a leader with character? It is widely understood that experience is a part of the character-building process, but many people with extensive management and leadership experience never develop much character. While ethics and morality are not one and the same, understanding how people develop morally helps us to understand character development, and it also clarifies why there is a need for professional and personal ethics.

The late Harvard professor Lawrence Kohlberg extensively studied moral development and found three general levels of morality: *preconventional*, *conventional*, and *postconventional*.[6] In his research, he found some similarities between the process of cognitive development and the process of moral development. Specifically, an individual develops sequentially from a lower level to a higher level, and he or she cannot reach a higher level without first comprehending and developing morality at the immediately preceding lower level.

He found that most young children are preconventional; they believe something is right simply because a person of authority says it is right. Someone at this level has little or no sense of right and wrong, but believes it is important to follow rules because doing so is personally beneficial. For example, a young child will do what her parents tell her to do, knowing that she will be rewarded if she does and held accountable or punished if she does not.

An adult who has not developed beyond this level might honestly report income to the Internal Revenue Service not because it is the right thing to do but because not doing so could result in financial penalties or prison. On the other hand, if pre-conventional individuals think they will not be caught, they would be comfortable underreporting income.

At the conventional level, people follow rules because they believe that order in society creates positive outcomes and they value such outcomes. For them, rules exist for the practical purpose of ensuring equity and efficiency in the world. Individuals at the conventional level, for example, might believe it is good to obey the law and stop their car at a stoplight because doing so reduces the number of automobile accidents. Additionally, they may believe they should honestly report taxable income to the Internal Revenue Service not just because they wish to avoid punishment but also because they believe that funding national defense, infrastructure, education, and other programs is necessary for maintaining order in society. They understand there will be sufficient revenues only if people pay taxes.

People who have reached the highest level of moral development, postconventional, believe that morality and virtue have intrinsic worth. They believe it is important to be honest not because doing so may have a positive outcome but because the truth, in and of itself, has value. This level of moral development is analogous to one's recognition that gold or diamonds have high worth, while gold-colored metal and rhinestones that only look like gold and diamonds do not.

For post-conventional individuals, virtues such as honesty, kindness, loyalty, compassion, and courage are valuable in and of themselves. They believe that regardless of outcome, the truth is better than a lie, kindness is better than cruelty, loyalty is better than betrayal, compassion is better than indifference, and courage is better than cowardice. Virtues have positive value and are assets, while the absence of virtue is a liability.

Kohlberg's research led him to believe that most people do not move beyond the conventional level of moral development.[7] Not every adult reaches the conventional level of moral development, however. For example, a businesswoman whose decisions are guided primarily by what the markets and law will allow, rather than by what is in the best interest of the society, is operating at the preconventional level. She is guided not by virtue or by what she believes makes society function in a more orderly way, but by what she believes she can get away with while avoiding cost or punishment.

When government officials violate a law and act in their own self-interest, rather than the public's interest, believing they will not get caught, then they are acting at the preconventional level. Former Illinois governor Rod Blagojevich exhibited the preconventional level of moral development when he engaged in criminal acts that included attempted extortion, conspiracy to commit extortion, soliciting of bribes, wire fraud, and conspiracy to solicit and accept bribes. One example was his offer to appoint a US senator to fill the seat vacated by President-Elect Barack Obama in exchange for items that would benefit him personally.[8]

Like a child who has not yet developed a moral compass, Governor Blagojevich conducted government business in a way that reflected zero sense of right or wrong. And like a child who believes he won't be punished if his parents do not see what he has done, Rod Blagojevich believed he was clever enough to keep his wrongdoings out of public sight. He erroneously believed he would not get caught and did not realize that his conversations pertaining to his illegal behavior were being recorded. Had he known he was being recorded, he likely would have behaved differently.

Even though research suggests that the majority of people do not ever move beyond the conventional level of moral development, when asked, most people say that they want to be ethical and believe they are more ethical than others. This disparity between what people believe about themselves and how they behave is likely the result of people not giving a great deal of thought to what it means to be ethical. That is terribly unfortunate. As a society, we would have greater character if more of us made the effort to understand the intrinsic value of a virtuous and principled life.

More than once I have received pushback in my endeavors to strengthen ethical standards in the public sector. When I introduced gift-ban legislation in the US House of Representatives, many of my colleagues expressed opposition to the bill, saying that they could not be influenced by a gift. They were completely sincere in their belief. But I knew that people were more likely to be persuaded when they were given a soft drink and peanuts. When I began working to strengthen ethics provisions at the Farm Credit Administration (FCA), I was told by a very upstanding colleague that ethics are a matter of opinion. To the contrary, the study of ethics and the adoption of ethical standards date back centuries.

There are professional ethicists who dedicate their entire careers to this field of work. Well-developed philosophies of morality and ethics underlie the study and understanding of ethics, and there is broad agreement regarding what constitutes ethical behavior. Even a basic understanding of these works will help one build character and make better decisions.

Over the centuries, philosophers have approached ethics and morality in a number of ways. Three of the more prominent theories are *virtue*, *deontological*, and *utilitarian*.

Virtue philosophers believe that good qualities lie within us and we intuitively know right from wrong. Aristotle believed that making a habit of behaving with virtue will lead one to become a person of virtue. If someone consistently shows kindness to others, he or she will become a kind person, or if someone consistently acts with courage, he or she will become a courageous person.

My husband is a man of courage. Don is a retired fighter pilot who served in both the US Navy and Air National Guard. His story of the first time he landed an airplane on an aircraft carrier exemplifies how courage can be built. He is very honest in acknowledging that he was more than a little tense as he was flying his A-7 on final approach toward the carrier. He experienced both relief and exhilaration as his landing gear touched down and the tailhook caught the cable for the very first time. According to Don, each of his succeeding carrier landings became easier, mentally and physically. He behaved with courage and became a man of great courage.

Being courageous does not mean that we no longer have fear; it means that we face a challenge despite our fear. My husband is brave, but he is not fearless. I once asked him if he was nervous the first time he refueled his fighter plane in air; he grinned and said he was nervous the last time he refueled his fighter plane in air. Becoming a person of character is not a single high-jump event but a marathon that is accomplished one step at a time.

Another moral theory, deontology, is based on the belief that we all have a duty to be principled and honest in our actions. *Deon* is the Greek word for duty. The well-known German deontological philosopher Immanuel Kant believed that we have the duty to show respect to others. He argued that people should never be treated as a means to an end but as an end in and of themselves. And our behavior should be guided by the principle that we must treat others as we would want to be treated. For example, he believed that we must never tell an untruth to another person because we have a duty to always be honest in what we say to others.

Kant taught that it would be wrong to deviate from the principle of honesty; according to him, we always have a duty to be honest, even if we believe that doing so could have negative consequences. This deontological approach to ethics clearly has merit because it recognizes there is value in principle-based decision-making, but it can have pragmatic shortcomings.

Following Kant's reasoning, for example, one could argue that the people who ran the Underground Railroad were not behaving ethically because they were not being honest and transparent about their actions. If asked what they were doing, according to Kant, they would have to be forthcoming and honest in their response, even though doing so could cost others their lives. That would completely ignore the larger issue of slavery, the immorality of owning another person, and the morality of working to end it.

I think one of the keys to ethical decision-making is acknowledging that there are often conflicts between and among virtues and principles, requiring us to use a multifaceted analysis of the actions we are considering. And we are not thorough in our analysis if we do not consider how our decisions might affect others.

This leads us to utilitarianism, another philosophical theory of ethics. The central tenet of this approach is impact on others, and I believe it is particularly relevant to decision-making and leadership in business and government. How our decisions affect other people should always be of concern. For example, in the development of federal tax policy, Congress conducts analyses of how changes in the tax code will impact people at various income levels. Such analysis is critical to the development of fairness of policy. Unfortunately, some lawmakers choose to ignore the analyses and instead support policies based on ideology or political support or even less acceptable reasons.

These various philosophies of morality are all consistent, at least to some degree, with the principles of democracy. In a democratic society, we believe that no individual should ever be treated as a means to an end and that everyone should have equal opportunity to participate in the self-governing process. This recognizes the importance of a policy-making process that is fair, as well as outcomes that are fair.

Learning about philosophical theories of ethics is useful because such knowledge can help us more honestly analyze an ethics dilemma. The succeeding chapter includes an application of these philosophies for addressing ethical dilemmas.

Most people are not ethical purists. We know humans are not perfectly objective when it comes to decision-making. Our decisions are influenced by a variety of factors, including psychological issues and biases. Understanding the psychology of how we make decisions can help us make better choices.

In the 1990s, there emerged a field of study focused on how and why people behave ethically or unethically when faced with various ethical dilemmas. This field, called *behavioral ethics*, seeks to find the answers to the "why" of ethical or unethical decision-making. Its research and teachings include psychology, cognitive science, neuroscience, and evolutionary biology. It is different from philosophy because it focuses on how people actually behave rather than on how they ought to behave. Understanding how we make ethical decisions helps us make more ethical decisions.[9]

Research in behavioral ethics highlights that people are emotional and our emotions impact everything we do. Most of the time, we don't give much thought to the "why" of our decisions, and often when we try to analyze why we do something, we aren't very objective. Marketers who know how to tap into our emotional needs and biases can be very successful at designing and selling us products. For example, few of us choose a car based solely on its ability to provide reliable transportation to and from our chosen destinations. Most of us don't buy shoes simply to protect our feet. And even the food we eat is often chosen to meet social and psychological needs as much as nutritional needs. Our product choices are heavily influenced by our families, our peers, and advertising.

Just as emotional needs and biases influence our purchasing decisions, they also influence other behaviors, including how we respond to ethics dilemmas or whether we even recognize an ethics dilemma when we're confronted with one. Trying to understand human behavior is a complex proposition. Why, for example, might people be more easily persuaded if they eat peanuts and drink Pepsi while they are reading promotional material? I have never been able to find a definitive answer to that question, but it seems logical that it would be the result of an association of the reading material with the pleasure of snacking. The peanuts and Pepsi may create a good feeling that is then associated with the promotional material.

Research in the field of behavioral ethics has found that people often have what is referred to as a *conformity bias*. Their behavior is influenced by and conforms with the behavior of others around them. For example, if a salesman works with other salespeople who pad their expense reports, he may view it as the norm and pad his own expense account.

Whatever the cause of our biases, it is important to understand that we are consistently being influenced in ways that are not apparent and that can lead to less than optimal decision-making. The better we understand ourselves, the more likely we are to make better choices. And if we all make better choices individually, we will be stronger as a nation.

Another challenge we face in decision-making is personal bias. We confront every situation with predispositions based on who we are and what we have experienced. This leads us to make attributions about events and people that, in part, reflect what we think we know rather than what is real or true. Each of us has experiences from our past that we draw upon to help us understand what is taking place in our current surroundings. Doing so can help us more efficiently figure out what we are confronting and what we should do. For example, when we are driving a car and approach a traffic light that turns from green to yellow, we know it will soon be turning red, and we respond accordingly. We don't give the situation conscious thought because we have had the same experience before. Our reaction to the changing light is automatic.

Our interpretation of past experiences become stored in our minds as a mental structure, or schema. Interpretations of multiple experiences are schemata. When we confront a new situation, we tend to see it in the context of our past experiences. We don't have the time or motivation to look at the new situation with all its complexity. Based on our past experiences, we have our own individual schema that influences the attributions we make about the new situation and the people who are a part of it. This helps us to simplify decision-making, but it also causes us to make mistakes in our perceptions.

Another memorable story from my husband's flying experiences illustrates well the problem of misperceptions. In addition to serving as a pilot in the military, he also flew for a major airline, retiring at the rank of captain. As a commercial pilot, he flew both domestic and international routes. During one of his flights from India to Germany, a flight attendant came to the cockpit to let the pilots know a passenger appeared to be experiencing cardiac arrest. Following official procedure, she asked for permission to use the plane's defibrillator on the passenger. My husband authorized her to do so and then suggested she first make a public announcement to ask if there were any doctors on board. The flight attendant responded by looking him squarely in the eyes and stating, "We're doctors."

He had never knowingly flown with flight attendants who were also medical doctors, and his schema caused him to make an incorrect assumption. That experience certainly makes the point that we should not prejudge the breadth of another person's interests, experiences, credentials, or skills based on what we see on one specific occasion. But it is what humans do.

For example, research shows that a fair number of voters are skeptical about female candidates' qualifications for serving in high public office. Professional campaign consultants have advised me against appearing with my husband at certain campaign events because voters will sometimes perceive the husband to be the candidate rather than the spouse of a female candidate.

On more than one occasion when my husband has been campaigning with me, voters have directed their questions to him even though I was the person running for office. To the contrary, when I have flown with him on his commercial flights, never once did someone confuse me for a pilot or a medical doctor. Sometimes after he had landed the plane and taxied to the gate, however, I would be standing just behind the bulkhead waiting for him to finish his paperwork, and deplaning passengers would mistake me for a flight attendant. They would quite graciously thank me for the great service. It was flattering, but I was never sure what to do. So I would just reply, "And thank you for flying with us!"

We draw all kinds of conclusions about people we meet based on very limited information, such as the community in which they live, the kind of car they drive, the style of clothes they wear, or the firmness of their handshake. We also make assumptions about people based on their gender and race. Sometimes our assumptions are positive and sometimes they are negative, and much of the time our assumptions contain errors.

The schemata we develop lead us to have unconscious biases about other people. And when we misperceive other people's abilities or motives, we increase the likelihood of treating them in a way that may not be fair to them or to others. The better we understand our biases, the greater the likelihood of making good and fair decisions. There have been a large number of studies showing the impact biases have on behavior, and they are quite relevant to understanding why ethical people often make unfair and unethical decisions.

Gender bias has been identified in numerous studies. In recent research on presentations made at a professional meeting on internal medicine, it was found that men more frequently used a doctor's professional title when introducing male presenters than when introducing female presenters. The specific findings were that men used the title *doctor* 72.4 percent of the time when introducing male doctors but only 49.2 percent of the time when introducing female doctors. Women used the title *doctor* approximately 95.0 percent of the time when introducing both male and female doctors.[10] In another recent study, researchers analyzed the transcripts of oral arguments of cases argued before the US Supreme Court. Their analysis showed that female justices are interrupted at disproportionate rates by their male colleagues.[11]

The Barbara Lee Family Foundation has funded research on how voter preferences differ for male and female candidates. The research shows that voters will support a male candidate if they don't like him but think he is qualified. But the voters have a higher standard when it comes to voting for female candidates. They are not as likely to vote for a woman unless two criteria are met: they must like her and think she is qualified. The research also found that men are generally assumed to be qualified, but women must prove they are.[12]

It is not just women who have to deal with biases, however. In research conducted on male facial traits and CEOs, it was found that the faces of CEOs have characteristics that subjects identified as a look of "competence." They also found that executive compensation was positively correlated to the look of "competence" ratings. But there has never been any finding in research that shows one's facial characteristics are related to competence.[13]

There is an exercise I like to use in the classroom to help improve awareness of personal biases. I state various professions and ask the students to identify the first image that comes to mind. For example, what are the characteristics of the person you imagine when you hear each of the following: steelworker, fighter pilot, doctor, nurse, teacher, school superintendent, garbage collector, lawyer, artist, professor, politician, police officer, and hairdresser? I continue the exercise by asking the students to identify what biases might be reflected in each image. In making the conscious effort to identify the images and associated biases these words evoke, we can begin to understand our perceptions and misperceptions pertaining to gender, race, and other characteristics.

If we have an interest in understanding the extent of our nation's unconscious biases, we might ask ourselves the following questions. Why are less than 10 percent of Fortune 500 companies headed by female CEOs?[14] Why have the voters of the United States never elected a woman to serve as president? What is the likelihood that a woman who has been married three times, runs casinos and beauty pageants, and has had six business bankruptcies would be elected president of the United States?

The better we understand ourselves, the easier it will be for us to open our minds, become more objective, and treat others more fairly. This increased awareness can also help us become more honest and ethical in navigating the world.

No matter how much we want to be fair and open-minded, we all have biases, and it is important for us to make our best effort to understand them. When we make the wrong attributions about other people's motives and capabilities, we increase the likelihood that we will treat them unfairly. In the workplace, misattributions often lead to the hiring or promotion of someone who is less qualified than others being considered for the job. At the ballot box, voters often elect the less capable candidate. Obviously, these kinds of wrong decisions impact more than the decision-makers. When we put less qualified people in charge, we pay the price of performing below our potential. This is true for businesses, for charitable organizations, and for government, and in all cases, it is costly. There is always a cost to bad decisions.

We will be better as individuals and as a society if we open our minds and seek truth and if we also commit ourselves to caring about others. Doing so will lead us to more honest and effective decision-making, because the truth leads us to more informed and better decisions. And when we care about others, we make the effort to understand their perspectives, which helps us find common ground and more workable solutions. And we will be upholding the values laid forth in the Declaration of Independence and the US Constitution.

THREE

—⁓—

THE HABIT OF LEADING
WITH CHARACTER

Dr. Martin Luther King's leadership reaffirmed the promise of our democracy: that everyday people, working together, have the power to change our government and our institutions for the better.

THE HONORABLE MARIA CANTWELL[1]

IN MY ROLE AS A professor of ethics, I am never at a loss for a relevant news account of someone in a high place behaving badly. Every day, it seems, there is some real-time revelation in the media about a public official or business leader engaging in an unethical or illegal way. I have found it important to not forget there are also examples of great leaders who used their talents in ways that made us better. As Senator Maria Cantwell so eloquently states, Dr. Martin Luther King Jr. was a leader who exemplified how everyday people can use the power of democracy to build a stronger America and world.

One can only imagine what a much-better world it would be if everyone put ethics front and center and made a serious commitment to developing ethical habits. There would be greater trust among people, businesses, and nations; we would all make better decisions built upon integrity and fact; and we would be more likely to find peaceful solutions to conflicts. We would waste fewer resources because we would be more likely to do things right the first time. When we make ethics a priority, we can make more thoughtful choices based on what we know rather than on what we wish the facts to be. And we won't burn as many bridges that have to be rebuilt because we will know how to work together with people whose trust we have earned.

I believe that the United States, from its very beginning, aspired to the higher calling of doing the right thing. The principles of democracy as laid forth in our Constitution, including the Bill of Rights, reflect a genuine commitment to integrity in the governing process and to the rights of the individual. On the world stage, we have not always been perfect. But we have regularly demonstrated upright and thoughtful leadership, and we became a nation of character. Allies and adversaries developed an understanding of what we stand for, and they knew there would be an underlying consistency in our dealings with them.

Our integrity and reliability earned us the trust of many governments and people around the globe, and that contributed to making us a dominant international force. Over the years, other nations have turned to us for leadership, in part because we have built economic and military might but also because we are principled in our commitment to liberty and justice and individual rights. Their trust in us makes us even stronger.

We must all recognize that trust is not something that is set in stone; it must be earned and re-earned, again and again. In a Gallup poll of 134 countries, it was found that median approval of US leadership had dropped 18 percentage points from 2016 to 2017.[2] Additionally, Pew Research Center polling found a significant drop in confidence of US presidential leadership from 2016 to 2018.[3]

If we want to continue our legacy as a world leader, then we have no choice but to insist that leaders at the highest levels in government and industry lead with a consistency of integrity and honor. As Aristotle taught, when we make a habit of behaving with virtue, we become a person of virtue. By extension, a nation that leads with character becomes a country of character, and that builds international trust, which makes us stronger. Very simply, good habits are better than bad habits. They are better for individuals and families, as well as for businesses, not-for-profits, and communities. They are also better for our country. Developing good and ethical habits is essential to character development.

We are more likely to make principled decisions when we anticipate ethics conflicts and prepare ourselves for dealing honestly with errant temptations.[4] I believe that candid introspection and analysis help us anticipate and prepare for conflicts. In other words, it is important to know who you are and to be true to yourself.

Character-based leadership requires an honorable and credible reason for being. The preamble to our Constitution gave the United States of America its purpose: forming a more perfect union, establishing justice, assuring domestic tranquility, providing for the common defense, promoting general welfare, and securing liberty to endure for future generations.

CHARACTER-DRIVEN PURPOSE

Our purpose must be character driven. A worthy purpose and a clear mission are essential to effective long-term, honorable leadership. Most successful, well-run organizations have formal mission statements that define and clarify their purpose, or reason to be. Mission statements establish the foundation for setting long-term and short-term goals, as well as developing the strategy for achieving those goals.

Well-thought-out, well-developed mission statements provide both operational and ethical focus, and they also establish parameters. An organization's values and principles should also be encompassed in the statement, and it is best to state them explicitly, rather than implicitly. Following are six mission statements presented as examples. The first three statements are for cabinet-level departments of the federal government, and the second three are from the business sector. Together they represent entities with quite different purposes, and they are each succinct yet complete in defining and clarifying purpose. I selected this variety of organizations' statements to show that regardless of an entity's pursuits, ethics can be integral to mission and performance.

Government Agency Mission Statements

Department of State

Vision: On behalf of the American people we promote and demonstrate democratic values and advance a free, peaceful, and prosperous world.

Mission: The U.S. Department of State leads America's foreign policy through diplomacy, advocacy, and assistance by advancing the interests of the American people, their safety and economic prosperity.[5]

Department of Defense

The Department of Defense provides the military forces needed to deter war and ensure our nation's security.[6]

Department of Health and Human Services

It is the mission of the U.S. Department of Health & Human Services (HHS) to enhance and protect the health and well-being of all Americans. We fulfill that mission by providing for effective health and human services and fostering advances in medicine, public health, and social services.[7]

Corporate Mission Statements

Kellogg Company

Vision: To enrich and delight the world through foods and brands that matter.

Purpose: Nourishing families so they can flourish and thrive.[8]

Microsoft

Our mission is to empower every person and every organization on the planet to achieve more.[9]

Eli Lilly and Company

Purpose: Lilly unites caring with discovery to create medicines that make life better for people around the world.[10]

While each of these organizations has a different mission, all the missions include character components. They stand for something of value, and all their statements include pillars of character, as identified by the Josephson Institute. To illustrate, the following phrases taken from the six statements reflect the values of caring and responsibility for other people:

- "promote and demonstrate democratic values and advance a free, peaceful, and prosperous world"
- "to deter war and ensure our nation's security"
- "enhance and protect the health and well-being of all Americans"
- "nourishing families so they can flourish and thrive"
- "empower every person and every organization . . . to achieve more"
- "make life better for people around the world"

They also include philosophical virtues and principles. For example, the Department of State is committed to building and sustaining peace, prosperity, and democracy at home and abroad. Microsoft has a mission that includes empowering people to be their best. And the Kellogg Company and Eli Lilly are committed to people's health and well-being. These purposes encompass the virtue of compassion for others and the principle of treating others with respect and dignity.

Additionally, they all seek to ensure a positive impact on people's lives, which encompasses the philosophy of utilitarianism. The Kellogg Company has the goal not only of "nourishing families" but also of helping them to "flourish and thrive." The Department of State is committed to security and prosperity for American people, as well as others around the world.

Establishing a meaningful purpose provides guidance in the development of habits. Organizations' habits are more commonly referred to as *practices*, and they are typically based on the policies, both formal and informal, of the organization. An organization's habits are a direct reflection of its people, especially its leadership. As with individuals, organizations perform better when they adopt good habits. And just like with individuals, it takes effort and discipline to develop good habits. But it really is not terribly difficult to get in a routine of behaving ethically, and such efforts have their own rewards.

Organization mission statements are quite common, but few individuals take the time to write a personal one for themselves. Yet making the effort to think about one's purpose and formalizing it in a written statement can be very useful in building a successful career and living a successful life.

The highly successful entertainer and businesswoman Oprah Winfrey has publicly shared her personal mission statement. Clearly, it has provided guidance and focus and has contributed to her many achievements.

Oprah Winfrey's Personal Mission Statement

To be a teacher. And to be known for inspiring my students to be more than they thought they could be.[11]

Another highly successful business leader, Richard Branson, the founder of the Virgin Group, has a less serious mission statement. While lighthearted and simple, it recognizes the value of personal responsibility in learning from one's mistakes.

Richard Branson's Personal Mission Statement

To have fun in (my) journey through life and learn from (my) mistakes.[12]

Many years ago, I developed a mission statement for myself, based on the teachings of my family and the United Methodist Church. Over the years, it has helped me stay focused on what I believe has value.

My Personal Mission Statement

To honorably and ethically use my talents and skills to benefit family, friends, community, country, and world with the goal that all will be stronger for the efforts I make.

In my ethics classes, early in each semester I allot a small amount of class time for students to individually and confidentially write a description of who they are and whom they want to become. While technically not a mission statement, their answers to those two questions help clarify their thinking about their respective purposes in life. I never ask them to share what they have written, but I do ask them if they find the exercise useful. Their feedback is always positive. Many students have expressed that the exercise helps them identify and clarify their priorities, their personal values, and the contributions they want to make to the world. They also tell me it helps them establish values-based priorities.

While a mission statement is important, it is of value only if it is actually used for setting standards and limitations pertaining to choices and behaviors. Additionally, adopting a mission statement is just the first step in running an ethical organization or living an ethical life. One must also adhere to its values and principles in every decision that gets made. But even more is needed to ensure ethical decision-making and ethical behavior. Formal codes of ethics that establish specific parameters for behavior and are reflective of the values of the mission are also integral to ethical decision-making by organizations and individuals. Examples of such codes of ethics are presented in the two succeeding chapters.

Good decision-making is not inherent; it is learned. Making sound and ethical decisions requires an understanding of how to strategically frame and address challenges, including ethics dilemmas. Developing the habit of objectively analyzing the "rightness" of potential courses of action and then choosing the one that is most ethical lead us to better decisions and help build our character. Borrowing from the late University of Michigan professor LaRue Hosmer and his ethical-decision-making process, I propose using the following steps, with the potential to lead us all to better, more ethical decision-making.[13] The five-step approach presented here is a modified version of his method, but it includes his major variables.

Steps for Ethical Decision-Making

1. Define the ethics dilemma and the potential harm to vulnerable parties.
2. Gather additional information relevant to fully understanding the issue at hand.
3. Identify all reasonable alternatives.
4. Analyze each alternative using the following criteria:
   - Is the alternative virtuous?
   - Is the alternative principled?
   - How will the alternative impact each vulnerable party?
5. Choose the most ethical course of action based on the analysis.

This approach is consistent with strategic decision-making. Regardless of the situation, it is always important to define the problem or challenge and to gather all relevant information. It is also important to identify realistic alternatives. In step four, the focus is on analyzing how ethical each alternative is. This step includes the three philosophical approaches presented earlier: virtue, deontological, and utilitarian.

Regular implementation of these steps will help organizations and individuals develop the habit of ethical decision-making. I would also argue that doing so will build their character.

Following is a lighthearted and simple illustration of how this process can be applied. Two cousins, Bonnie and Liz, get together every Saturday for lunch at their local Bob Evans restaurant, where a coffee refill is free. Liz drives, and Bonnie buys lunch. They both like coffee, but as they are both quite frugal, Bonnie is the only one who orders coffee with her meal. After finishing lunch, she always asks for a coffee refill in a to-go cup, but she never drinks the second cup. Instead, when she leaves the restaurant, she takes it with her to the car and very discreetly gives it to her cousin Liz.

1. What is the dilemma? Bonnie must determine if it is honorable to buy only one cup of coffee and ask for the free refill for the purpose of giving it to Liz. She knows that when she asks for the refill, she is implying to the server that the second cup is for her.
2. Additional information that would be useful is the specific Bob Evans policy on free coffee refills, as well as the cost of the refill and the to-go cup.
3. Bonnie and Liz have three alternatives:
   - They can each order a cup of coffee.
   - One can order a cup of coffee and give the refill to the other.
   - One can order a cup of coffee and not give the refill to the other.
4. The virtuous and principled options are the ones that reflect integrity and transparency. Buying one cup of coffee, asking for a refill, and giving it to someone else is neither virtuous nor principled because Bonnie is implying the refill is for her. She is not being honest or transparent. From a utilitarian perspective, buying only one cup of coffee and giving the refill to someone else drives up the overall cost of coffee for Bob Evans. That cost then will be passed on to other customers, which is not fair to them. If Bonnie and Liz both order coffee, they are being principled and virtuous because they are not misleading the server. Additionally, they are not passing any costs on to Bob Evans or other customers. For similar reasons, it is virtuous and prin-

cipled to order one cup of coffee and not ask for a refill to be
shared with the other cousin.
5. Based on this analysis, the ethical options are to buy two cups of
coffee or one cup with no refill to be given to cousin Liz.

Taking advantage of a coffee refill policy at Bob Evans may seem a bit trivial.
It's only a cup of coffee and a to-go cup. The action, however, suggests that integrity can be bought for the price of a cup of coffee. The issue is not the coffee;
it is the way the coffee is acquired. Virtue and principle are not to be traded for
personal gain of any amount.

There are parallels between this situation and ethics dilemmas faced by
those in public service. If local police officers accept free coffee from a local
coffee shop, will they then be more likely to patrol its neighborhood? Are they
trading a higher level of security in that neighborhood for a cup of coffee, and
at what cost to the people of other neighborhoods?

What if I told you that Bonnie and Liz are highly ethical but grew up during the Great Depression? I know these women well, and they were taught by
their parents to be very frugal and not to waste food or drink. Because of their
upbringing, they both believe that it would be wasteful for them not to take
the free refill.

While it is my opinion that the only ethical course of action for them is to
not ask for a free refill and share it, I also believe that I have a responsibility to
be understanding of others' perspectives. As children of the Depression, they
believe they are being responsible by not wasting a free cup of coffee. While it
is perfectly appropriate for me to analyze the propriety of their actions, it would
not be ethical for me to ignore the circumstances in their backgrounds that
have influenced their perspectives. Empathy and understanding are attributes
of character and are important in our personal lives.

These characteristics are also important to democracy, because we are best
served when we have legitimate trust in the process and in our leaders. When
we work to understand the circumstances of others, we can build trust.

It is very disconcerting that public trust in government to do the right thing
is low. In Gallup polling, public approval of Congress has consistently been
averaging only 30 percent since the mid-1970s.[14] This lack of confidence in our
public leaders should give us all concern.

Even though some public officials have given us reason to lose confidence
in our government, my years in Congress and the executive branch taught
me that many, if not most, public servants are honorable people. There are

numerous leaders across the country who have well-developed and noble missions for their lives and careers. Just like in any line of work, however, there are both ethically motivated and not-so-ethically motivated people who work in government. Some public officials operate at a preconventional level of ethical development; some operate at a conventional level; and some operate at a postconventional level. Unfortunately, the unethical behavior of even one public official can affect the confidence we have in our democracy.

As I stated earlier in the book, I have often received pushback from colleagues for my efforts to elevate ethical standards in government. Even highly principled colleagues have expressed their belief that ethics are a matter of opinion. But a person who thinks that does not understand what ethics are. Many people confuse ethics with moral or religious beliefs, which are very personal.

Since ethics are not morality or religion, it is possible for people who hold different moral and religious beliefs to agree on what constitutes ethical behavior in many different circumstances. The entities who adopted the six mission statements above all have different functions and purposes, yet they share well-founded values. These common threads illustrate that ethics and character are something different from morality, religion, or a matter of opinion.

The development of ethical habits is essentially an objective and analytical process, and the results can be quite impactful. The definition of ethics provided in the first chapter—"well-founded standards of right and wrong that prescribe what humans ought to do, usually in terms of rights, obligations, benefits to society, fairness, or specific virtues"—establishes the parameters for analyzing whether a potential action is ethical. We can objectively analyze any potential course of action with regard to whether it violates or protects others' rights, disregards or upholds our obligations to others, harms or helps society, is unjust or fair to impacted parties, and is dishonorable or virtuous and principled.

Ethics dilemmas can be complex and, therefore, confusing. Knowing ourselves and being prepared to confront a dilemma or temptation can help us make the kinds of decisions of which we can be proud. Ethical lapses are not unique to any one line of work or sector of the population. Regardless of profession or demographics, we all have a role to play in strengthening our nation's character.

The next two chapters contain analyses of professional codes of ethics for those who work in the federal government and in the business sector. For this book, I chose not to include state or local government ethics codes and laws. Since they are different in each state, it would be rather unwieldy to cover all of them. The purpose of this book is to show why specific types of ethics laws and restrictions are necessary for preserving and protecting democracy rather than to present a comprehensive analysis of the totality of ethics laws. I also limit the analysis regarding business ethics to the kinds of restrictions that are relevant to upholding democratic values.

Developing an understanding of ethics in government and business is very useful in increasing ethical awareness and developing ethical habits. We will never universally agree on religion or morality, but we know from research and from personal experiences that there exist widely shared values pertaining to character, including the underlying principles of democracy, that provide a foundation for ethical decision-making in government and the private sector. Research findings confirm that active, strong ethics programs with education, training, and enforcement are most effective in helping organizations stay on track and avoid the cost associated with ethical crises.[15]

Understanding why certain kinds of ethics codes are relevant to democratic values can help us collectively agree upon and aspire to a more ethical government and society in the name of the democracy we cherish.

FOUR

—ɯ—

ETHICS AND DEMOCRACY

*My fellow Americans: ask not what your country can do for you—ask what
you can do for your country.*

PRESIDENT JOHN F. KENNEDY[1]

I WAS EIGHT YEARS OLD and in the third grade when my family sat in front
of our RCA black-and-white console television set and listened to President
John F. Kennedy speak these words during his inaugural address in January
1961. I thought he was telling us to be respectful to our country and the world,
to work hard and make a meaningful contribution, to be truthful, and to not
make messes with the expectation that others will clean up after us.

It is almost six decades later, and I still think that was, at least, a part of
his message. Responsibility, commitment to others, integrity, and hard work
are all essential to fulfilling the mission the founding fathers set forth in the
Constitution "to form a more perfect Union, establish Justice, insure domestic
Tranquility, provide for the common defence, promote the general Welfare, and
secure the Blessings of Liberty to ourselves and our Posterity."

Honest, capable leadership is central to a nation's character and strength,
but when all is said and done, a democracy is only as strong as its citizenry. We
the people are stronger when we take seriously the responsibilities we have to
our community and the larger society and when we face life's challenges with
integrity. Accountability and transparency are central to integrity, which is central to democracy. There must be integrity in the way we enact and administer

public policy. For that to happen, there must be integrity among the people, as well as in leadership.

I believe there are many threats to good government, but none is greater than conflicts between the interests of those in power and the interests of the public good. Integrity in government is a broad concept, and it demands transparency. It also requires a political system that establishes and enforces laws that minimize conflicts of interest while maximizing the potential for serving the public good. This is not easy, and it requires diligence from all of us, not just our leaders.

Running a government is not like running a business. Businesses exist to generate a profit while providing a product that serves the needs or wants of the customer. Governments exist to provide order and security for a society. In democracy, everyone has a role in making the government work. Citizens have a responsibility to pay their taxes, to not abuse public programs or public property, and to respect the rights of others. They also have an obligation to become informed and stay informed on candidates, public officials, and policy. We all share these responsibilities, and we should take them seriously.

Public employees work for their fellow citizens, whereas private sector employees work for the owners or shareholders of the business. While we all have a responsibility to conduct our work honestly and to the best of our abilities, public employees have a duty to broadly serve the public interest as well as to provide an honest day's work for an honest day's pay. At the heart of public service is a duty to others and to our democratic form of government. That is so for permanent career employees, as well as elected officials and political appointees.

When the personal interests of government employees, and especially of those who work in high-ranking and executive positions, conflict with the public's interests, integrity becomes compromised, and the very principles of a democratic government are undermined. When political leaders speak untruths and put their own interests above their country's interests, quite frankly, they make a mess. And cleaning up messes is costlier than doing things right the first time.

Some conflicts of interest are more obvious than others. In law, certain types of circumstances and acts are specifically defined as conflicts of interest, such as a public official's ownership of assets whose value could be impacted by the decisions she makes in her official capacity as an employee of the government. It is difficult, if not impossible, to be objective when making a work-related decision that could have a financial impact on oneself.

Yet, since we are all affected by budget decisions, tax policies, and many other public policy areas of civil law, there will always be people working for government who are broadly impacted by their own work as public servants. Also challenging to democracy are conflicts of interest that result from personal and professional friendships. Just as it is difficult to be unbiased about matters that impact ourselves, it can also be difficult to be unbiased about matters that impact our friends.

Other situations and acts are classified differently in our laws but in a generic sense are also conflicts of interest. Bribery is a criminal act that is generally not characterized as a conflict of interest in legal terms. But in a very real sense, it is probably the most audacious and flagrant example of such a conflict.

These conflicts can seriously undermine democracy. When a legislator takes money in exchange for a vote, it is quite clear the democratic process is compromised. When an executive branch employee takes money from a contractor in exchange for awarding him a government contract, the public's interest is compromised. And when a judge takes money in exchange for a favorable ruling, fairness of the judiciary is compromised. Accepting a bribe is a criminal act. It is also an act in which perpetrators choose the alternative they believe is in their own interest, rather than what is in the public's interest.

One of the most reprehensible cases involving public corruption and conflicts of interest was that involving high-profile Washington lobbyist Jack Abramoff. In total, twenty-one people, including Mr. Abramoff, other lobbyists, a member of Congress, officials in the Bush administration, and congressional staffers, pled guilty or were found guilty of various crimes, ranging from bribery to corruption.[2] Mr. Abramoff and his colleagues lavished public officials with expensive gifts, including concert tickets, luxury seats at Redskins games, and golf trips to Scotland, in exchange for helping Abramoff's clients. In every instance, someone in the government decided to serve the interests of the individuals involved rather than the interests of the citizenry. And in every instance, the democratic process and rights of equitable participation were undermined.

In the process of making and executing public law, we can reduce the potential for behavior that violates democratic principles by setting up procedures that encourage and support integrity and transparency. As presented previously, transparency is critical to the democratic process.

FINANCIAL DISCLOSURE

Toward the goal of improving transparency and reducing conflicts of interest, Congress passed the Ethics in Government Act of 1978. Since then, high-level officials in all three branches of the federal government are required to annually and publicly file financial disclosure statements. Among the items that must be reported are the following: "financial holdings and transactions in income-producing property and assets, such as stocks, bonds, mutual funds, and real property, as well as information on income, gifts, and reimbursements from private non-governmental sources."[3] All officials are required to file such statements, and they must also disclose much of the same information regarding their spouses and dependent children.

In addition to filing annual reports, high-ranking employees in Congress and the executive branch are also required to file periodic and expedited financial disclosure statements for certain circumstances. These disclosure reports are required of federal officials who purchase, sell, or exchange stocks, bonds, commodities futures, or other forms of securities that exceed $1,000. The Stop Trading on Congressional Knowledge Act, passed and signed into law in 2012, "affirms that all federal officials have a 'duty' of trust and confidentiality" and requires "public reporting within 30 days of receipt of notice of a covered transaction (but in no event more than 45 days after such transaction)."[4] This law helps protect the democratic process by prohibiting public officials from using nonpublic information to benefit themselves, at a potential cost to others who do not have access to the same information.

CODES OF ETHICS

With the goal of open and honest governance, legally binding codes of ethics have been adopted by governments at all levels. Each of the three branches of the US federal government has its own code of ethics. While they may not be perfect and are only effective when enforced, they are necessary for the democratic process to function. Even with these codes, too many public employees and officials still act in self-serving and sometimes illegal ways that harm the democratic process. Without the codes, however, the situation would be even worse.

To understand how an official government code of ethics works, it is important to understand its purpose. It is a professional protocol of standards that, when followed, increases the potential for better government and reduces the opportunity and probability of official actions that violate the underlying principles of democracy, as laid forth in our Constitution. Its purpose is not to establish morality for our citizens or to force all public employees to adopt and live by a specific set of morals.

The three branches were created to play independent and equal, but different, roles. They also have different authorities. Congress is charged with writing laws; the executive branch is charged with administering the laws;

and the judicial branch is charged with providing justice as conferred by the Constitution and Congress. But there are common issues of concern across the three branches and commonalities among their three official codes of ethics.

Even with this division of authorities, there is some overlap among the three branches. For example, the president has the power of the executive order, of signing or vetoing legislation passed by Congress, as well as impoundment authority that effectively negates congressional appropriations by withholding funds. Also, the vice president has the official tie-breaking role when the US Senate is deadlocked in a vote. And the federal courts can strike down a law passed by Congress or a presidential executive order if they determine it is unconstitutional.

Strong ethical standards are equally important to all three branches of government, but I think developing a workable code of ethics for Congress is more challenging than for the executive or judiciary. The citizenry has knowledge and experience useful to the policy-making process, and it is the specific responsibility of US senators and representatives to gather input and data from the people of their home states and across the country. This is necessary to the adoption of policies that reflect the needs and interests of the governed. In a democracy, direct interaction and relationship-building with the public are critical to a fair and informed legislative process.

But this direct interaction can make it difficult for lawmakers to remain objective. We know from research in the field of social psychology that personal relationships can be influential in ways that are not particularly democratic. This creates real challenges to ensuring that the process of gathering necessary information doesn't corrupt the process of writing fair and balanced legislation.

I think it is important for all of us, not just those who serve in high public office, to understand the principles and reasoning that underlie the codes of ethics for the three branches of the federal government. It allows us to better grasp why and how we must hold officials accountable in ways that uphold and strengthen our democracy. The major provisions of the codes of ethics for the three branches of the federal government are broadly presented in this chapter. My intent is not to provide a comprehensive, in-depth analysis of these ethics codes but rather to show how specific provisions in the codes are central to upholding democratic principles. A major purpose of these codes is protecting the values and tenets of democracy. I believe that understanding them helps clarify why democracy's very survival depends on ethical leadership.

When someone is elected or appointed to high office, we want that person to be competent, and we also want him or her to conduct the people's business in an honorable way. Our goal is not to find the most moral person to serve in office. Rather, we want to find someone who is highly capable and who also has a commitment to democracy and an understanding of the role ethics play in preserving and protecting democracy. Whether it is the legislative, executive, or judicial branch in which someone is serving, an appreciation of and commitment to government ethics is vital.

EXECUTIVE BRANCH

When President Obama nominated me to serve as a board member at the Farm Credit Administration, I was required to file a financial disclosure report of my husband's and my holdings and liabilities. I was also required to release our federal tax returns for review by the Office of Presidential Personnel. Such disclosure is a requirement of all candidates for high-ranking service in the federal executive branch.

The FCA is an independent prudential regulator charged with ensuring the safety and soundness of the Farm Credit System, which is comprised of private-sector lending institutions. As regulators, the board members have legal authorities and powers that impact the institutions in the system. It is in the public interest for there to be minimal conflict between potential benefits to a regulator and the long-term financial well-being of the system and the larger economy.

The primary purpose of the financial disclosure requirement is to determine if an appointee personally has any holdings or liabilities that could be impacted by the decisions he or she might make while carrying out the professional responsibilities of the position. If, for example, my husband or I had a loan from an institution in the Farm Credit System, there could be a conflict between what was in our financial interest and what was in the best interest of the lender, other borrowers, or the public.

We had never borrowed from a lending institution in the Farm Credit System, so we had no loans that could have created such a conflict. As I was preparing the financial disclosure documents, I wanted to also make sure we held no investments in businesses that had borrowed from the system. If we owned equity shares in a business that had acquired a loan from a system lender, I could potentially face a circumstance where my decisions as a regulator would impact my own personal finances.

Digging a little deeper into the financial records of firms in which we had invested, I discovered that we might have a potential conflict. We are strong proponents of renewable energy, and several years prior to my appointment, my husband had purchased equity shares in an ethanol production facility located in Nebraska. I asked him to conduct a thorough review of the refinery's finances. In doing so, he discovered that it had borrowed money from a Farm Credit lender. I immediately provided the loan information to the Farm Credit Administration Designated Agency Ethics Official (DAEO), who advised us that the equity shares must be liquidated.

We agreed with the DAEO. It could pose a real conflict of interest for us to own shares of stock in a business that had borrowed from a financial institution in the very system I would be overseeing and regulating. But selling the shares was not a realistic option. The stocks were not publicly traded, and we could not find a buyer. The ethics official then advised that my husband could gift the shares to a charity or to someone who was not a dependent child or a business partner. He very kindly and generously did so.

My husband and I grew up on family farms where money was always tight. As children, we were both taught how to stretch a dollar. We were also taught that when you are lucky enough to have a little extra money, that money should be invested, not spent. It was not easy to just give away those shares of stock. But we feel very fortunate to have been born and raised in the United States of America, and we believe that public service is a privilege. We also understand that integrity, transparency, and public trust are vital to a successful and enduring democracy.

Disclosure of tax returns helps to ensure that any taxes owed have been paid on time, and it also helps to determine if there may be any conflicts between one's financial interests and the public's interests. It is a requirement that protects the democratic process. I believe that any person who seeks or holds high office should be required to provide his or her tax returns for review. The president of the United States and anyone seeking the office of the presidency should not be exempted.

Apart from Donald Trump, every president since Jimmy Carter has done so. Richard Nixon released his tax returns, and Gerald Ford released a summary of his tax data.[5] I believe that we should expect nothing less from the person who holds the highest office in the land. Democracy works only when there is a level of transparency that ensures that public office holders do not have personal interests that could potentially conflict with the country's interests. As a nation of people who care about and benefit from living in a democratic society, we should make it a requirement.

My years of work in the federal government have provided me a bird's-eye perch for viewing the making and implementation of public policy. I have seen the honorable, the not-so-honorable, and the downright dishonorable. These observations have convinced me that formal ethics rules that minimize conflicts of interest and advance transparency and equity are crucial to successfully running a democratic government. I believe they are necessary for protecting the principles of our Constitution and for securing our position of international leadership.

The late J. Roland Pennock offered the following definition of democracy: "government by the people, where liberty, equality and fraternity are secured to the greatest possible degree and in which human capacities are developed to the utmost, by means including free and full discussion of common problems and interests."[6]

It is the antithesis of democracy for a government employee to put his or her own self-interests above the public's interests. Quite simply, such behavior is autocratic, not democratic. This applies to elected officials and political appointees as well as to career civil servants. A public employee merely giving the appearance of putting personal gain above the public good can generate mistrust in government institutions and undermine the democratic process. At its very core, democracy demands that public decisions be equitable in both process and outcome. And that requires a commitment to fairness and the public good.

The Declaration of Independence states that "all Men are created equal . . . with certain unalienable Rights" and "that to secure these Rights, Governments are instituted among Men, deriving their just Powers from the Consent of the Governed." In his Gettysburg Address, President Abraham Lincoln decreed "that government of the people by the people for the people, shall not perish from the earth."[7] When public employees have personal interests that conflict with the public's interests, the consent of the governed becomes threatened. We must do all we can to minimize conflicts of interest.

In a perfect democracy, every decision and action by the government would be objective and fair. But democracies are run by people encumbered with the many complexities of humanity. All of us, even individuals with the highest integrity, have feelings and personal biases that get in the way of our objectivity. It may be impossible to altogether eliminate conflicts of interest in public service, in business, or even in philanthropy. If we prohibited policy-makers from participating in any decisions that might impact someone they know or are related to, only robotic recluses could serve in public office.

We must recognize that public officials are like the rest of us. They have personal relationships with families and friends, and just like us, they tend to be more empathetic to the people they know. When we humans are confronted with dilemmas and issues that can impact the people we personally care about, we often view the circumstance through a lens that has been colored and shaped by our concern for them.

This empathy can be good for the democratic process because it helps policy-makers understand the real-life impacts their decisions can have on others. But when a public official's concern for the well-being of friends and family or those who have sought to curry favor via campaign contributions, gifts, or entertainment conflicts with the broader common good, the best interests of the public and the democracy itself are at risk.

Without adequate controls over these conflicts, the democratic process will crumble. That is why it is so important to draw a line that restricts government employees from having authority to make public decisions that directly impact their own personal wealth.

Also fundamental to democracy is transparency. It is not possible to have consent of the governed if the governing process is secretive or deceptive. As mentioned in chapter 1, the Constitution requires that Congress keep a journal, or record, of their proceedings. There was no radio, television, or internet when the Constitution was adopted at the end of the eighteenth century; the written word was the best way to ensure a level of transparency in the conducting of the people's business.

But our founding fathers also recognized that the executive and judicial branches must have transparency. Article II, Section 2 of the Constitution specifies that the president's high-ranking appointees be confirmed by the Senate, which is required to conduct business with transparency. And Article II, Section 3 requires the president to periodically provide to Congress information on the "State of the Union." The Sixth Amendment to the Constitution requires "a speedy and public trial, by an impartial jury" in all criminal prosecutions, thereby ensuring judicial branch transparency.

As long as there are humans, there will be perfidy. Cheaters are going to cheat. But when organizations and individuals make the commitment to uphold high ethical standards, unscrupulous behavior can be minimized, and honorable behavior can be maximized. Formal codes of ethics and the enforcement of such codes are critical to the democratic process.

There is no single right way for an organization or a government to build a culture of ethics and character. Even so, for many years, case studies have shown common practices among institutions that are successful in developing and implementing effective integrity programs. For example, effective ethics programs define meaningful values that guide decision-making and behavior. These values are widely communicated and understood throughout the organization, including by leadership at the highest levels, who also demonstrate a genuine and ongoing commitment to them. The organization's strategies and procedures support and enforce these stated values, and management integrates them into the routine channels of operations. Additionally, management is trained to incorporate ethics into day-to-day decision-making and implementation.[8]

More simply stated, a formal code of ethics that is enforced at the highest levels will improve ethical awareness and behavior. President George H. W. Bush understood the importance of ethics to democracy, and within a week of being sworn into office, he signed an executive order establishing the President's Commission on Federal Ethics Law Reform. Less than three months later, with a follow-up executive order, he established the Fourteen Principles of Conduct for Employees of the Executive Branch.[9]

In the aggregate, these Fourteen Principles serve the purpose of protecting the basic tenets necessary for successfully running and maintaining a democracy. In executing this code of ethical behavior, President George H. W. Bush sought to protect transparency and equity by eliminating conflicts of interest, including self-dealing, by those who run our government.

Fourteen Principles of Ethical Conduct for Executive Branch Employees

1. Public service is a public trust, requiring employees to place loyalty to the Constitution, the laws and ethical principles above private gain.
2. Employees shall not hold financial interests that conflict with the conscientious performance of duty.
3. Employees shall not engage in financial transactions using nonpublic Government information or allow the improper use of such information to further any private interest.
4. An employee shall not, except as permitted by subpart B of this part, solicit or accept any gift or other item of monetary value from any person or entity seeking official action from, doing business with, or conducting activities regulated by the employee's agency, or whose interests may be substantially affected by the performance or nonperformance of the employee's duties.
5. Employees shall put forth honest effort in the performance of their duties.

6. Employees shall not knowingly make unauthorized commitments or promises of any kind purporting to bind the Government.

7. Employees shall not use public office for private gain.

8. Employees shall act impartially and not give preferential treatment to any private organization or individual.

9. Employees shall protect and conserve Federal property and shall not use it for other than authorized activities.

10. Employees shall not engage in outside employment or activities, including seeking or negotiating for employment, that conflict with the official Government duties and responsibilities.

11. Employees shall disclose waste, fraud, abuse, and corruption to appropriate authorities.

12. Employees shall satisfy in good faith their obligations as citizens, including all just financial obligations, especially those—such as Federal, State, or local taxes—that are imposed by law.

13. Employees shall adhere to all laws and regulations that provide equal opportunity for all Americans regardless of race, color, religion, sex, national origin, age, or handicap.

14. Employees shall endeavor to avoid any actions creating the appearance that they are violating the law or the ethical standards set forth in this part. Whether particular circumstances create an appearance that the law or these standards have been violated shall be determined from the perspective of a reasonable person with knowledge of the relevant facts.[10]

These principles apply to all executive branch employees, except the president and vice president. Additionally, "in 18 U.S.C. Section 208, it is a crime for any United States government official in the Executive Branch to participate in a government matter that has a direct or indirect effect on that government official's financial interest. It is a crime. That statute applies to every single employee in the Executive Branch, except for two: the President and the Vice President."[11]

The reasons for these two exclusions are complex. The president is the head of the executive branch. This means that enforcement would be difficult, since employees at the Department of Justice are subordinate in rank to the president. Congress and the judiciary are also constitutionally limited in enforcement actions pertaining to the president. Additionally, regarding the gift restrictions, the Office of Government Ethics determined that the "President and Vice President may accept gifts from the public, as long as such gifts are not solicited or coerced, nor accepted in return for an official act."[12]

It is reasonable for us to expect, however, that the individuals elected to the highest office in the land would follow these principles. Presidents William J. Clinton, and George W. Bush all put their holdings into blind trusts. When Hillary Clinton began her own campaign for the presidency in 2007, she liquidated her blind trust and put the money into bank accounts, treasury notes, and mutual funds so that there would not even be the appearance of any potential conflicts of interest. President Obama's holdings of bank accounts, treasury notes, index funds, and college savings were not likely to pose a direct conflict of interest with the authorities he had as president, and it was felt that a blind trust was not necessary.[13] There are also times when protocol or etiquette make it appropriate for the president and vice president to accept gifts in their official capacities.

They all understood that the president of the United States has more power than any other executive branch employee, and they recognized the importance of the nation's highest public official complying with ethics standards that safeguard transparency and prohibit conflicts of interest to ensure that his or her actions will not undermine the democratic process. These presidents understood the importance of ethics to our national character. They honorably and appropriately put the public interest and our nation above their own self interests. We should expect no less from our president or vice president.

They may also have remembered the controversy when President Gerald Ford selected Nelson Rockefeller to be his vice president. Mr. Rockefeller was a successful businessman who had accumulated considerable wealth, and there was concern that his holdings would present a conflict with his official duties. The Senate held two sets of hearings in the fall of 1974, and the Joint Committee on Internal Revenue Taxation audited his 1963–1973 federal income tax returns. In addition to disclosing his holdings and tax returns, Mr. Rockefeller offered to put his holdings in a blind trust.[14] The committee determined that Mr. Rockefeller's candor regarding the specifics of his holdings and tax returns would allow Congress and the public to monitor his business activities and determine if there were any conflicts in interests.

A president should never place his or her own interests above the nation's interests. Doing so does not make America great. A president who is truly committed to America puts his or her country first. Noncompliance with basic ethical principles chips away at our democracy, and that is un-American.

Every one of these Fourteen Principles is important to the ethical running of our government. But a violation of certain principles will pose a more direct threat to our democratic process than would a violation of others.

For example, the first principle requires employees to place loyalty to the Constitution, the laws, and ethical principles above private gain. The second principle states that an executive branch employee shall not hold financial interests that create a conflict with the conscientious performance of duty. Principle fourteen prohibits employees from engaging in any action that even gives the appearance that they are in violation of the law or ethical standards set forth. When a public official chooses to defy any of these principles, he or she is undermining the very basic democratic principle of equal access to participation in the governing process. It would be illegal for any executive branch employee, except the president and vice president, to violate these principles.

As an example, a former postmaster general was fined $27,550 to settle a conflict-of-interest complaint that resulted from a recommendation he made to the US Postal Service's board of governors. When the board was deciding whether to enter into a strategic alliance between the Postal Service and a soft drink company, he advised in favor of the partnership. But he just happened to own shares of stock in the soft drink company, creating an opportunity for him to personally gain from the alliance.[15]

In another case of ethical failure, a contracting officer for the General Services Administration (GSA) directed over $11.5 million in contracts to a company that employed her husband. Because of these contracts, her husband received raises and a Jaguar from his employer. She ultimately pled guilty to violating conflict of interest laws, paid $161,000 in restitution, and served 180 days in home confinement and five years of probation.[16]

In both cases, these federal employees not only placed private gain above ethics principles, but they also likely made decisions that were not in the public's best interest. Was the strategic alliance between the US Postal Service and the soft drink company the best alternative for the American people? Did the GSA award contracts to the company that provided the greatest value for the cost? The answer to both questions is likely no. If the individuals in these two cases believed that a fair and transparent process would have had the same results, there would have been no incentive to rig the system.

It is easy to understand how such conflicts of interest undercut the core values of democracy and, therefore, why the Fourteen Principles of Ethical Conduct prohibit executive branch employees from holding assets that conflict with their responsibilities to the public. Presidents and vice presidents should be held to no less a standard than subordinates who have far less power in the running of our democracy.

If we imagine a president engaging in the behaviors described in the above scenarios, the issue becomes very clear. Most of us would agree that a president who owns an interest in a soft drink company should not be allowed to approve a contract for the US government to purchase soft drinks from that company. And we would likely agree that a president awarding a government contract to a company owned by a member of her or his own family would be a violation of the democratic principle of fair access.

If a government official owned hotels and golf clubs, would it be appropriate for her to schedule official government meetings at those hotels and clubs? Would it be appropriate for lobbyists with interests before the government employee's agency to stay at her hotels or to buy memberships in her clubs? I think we can all agree that these actions are inappropriate, because she is using her office for public gain and the lobbyists will have an unfair advantage over competitors, as well as the general public. This is analogous to a lobbyist buying a meal for a member of Congress, but on a much larger scale.

Principle eight prohibits federal employees from giving preferential treatment to any private organization or individual, because in a democracy, there should be equal access to participation, including in the awarding of government contracts. Additionally, the members of a president's security detail would also be staying at the hotel or clubs, all at taxpayer expense.

One could reasonably argue that if the federal government makes payments to a business owned by the president in order to cover the lodging for security detail members, it is in violation of the domestic Emoluments Clause. In these instances, the president would be receiving payment from the federal government. Included in Article II, Section 1 of the Constitution is the following: "The President shall, at stated Times, receive for his Services, a Compensation, which shall neither be increased nor diminished during the Period for which he shall have been elected, and he shall not receive within that Period any other Emoluments from the United States, or any of them." This Constitutional restriction is important for ensuring that the president's decision-making is not compromised by personal financial interests.

Presidential meetings with foreign dignitaries also carry additional concerns, if such meetings are held at a business the president owns. Under the foreign Emoluments Clause, in Article I, Section 9 of the Constitution, acceptance of earnings or pay from a "foreign State" must receive congressional approval. If a president is receiving food and lodging payments from a foreign government, that poses a serious conflict of interest. Official foreign policy should never be influenced by a president's potential to generate personal income from dealings with a foreign government or entity.

In the context of the ethical decision-making process presented in chapter 3, every one of these examples violates the democratic principles that lie at the very core of who we are as a nation. Public officials have a duty to conduct official business with transparency and in a way that places value on the best interests of the public.

In democracy, it matters *how* a president conducts the people's business. If the manner of governing is not fair and honest, then it is not a democratic process.

We have both a right and a responsibility to assess how our leaders, especially those at the highest levels, conduct our public business. And when they are not upholding even the most basic of democratic principles, we must demand either a change in their actions or a change in our leadership. Our future depends upon it.

I would argue that just because the president is technically not covered by the Fourteen Principles, he or she is not exempt from the standards established in these principles. Article II, Section 1 of the Constitution requires the president to take the following oath before being sworn into office: "I do solemnly swear (or affirm) that I will faithfully execute the Office of President of the United States, and will to the best of my Ability, preserve, protect, and defend the Constitution of the United States." Defending the Constitution includes promoting "the general Welfare," as stated in the preamble. It should be clear to all of us that a president who puts his or her financial interests above the people's interests is not promoting the general welfare and, therefore, is not upholding the Constitution.

Like any other federal employee, the president of the United States works for and is beholden to us, the citizens of the United States. And because he or she has more power than any other executive branch employee, unethical behavior on his or her part is even more damaging to our democratic process than on the part of another federal employee.

A number of federal agencies have ethics codes and policies that are even more stringent than the Fourteen Principles. For example, agencies that are classified as independent even though they are a part of the executive branch are generally statutorily required to operate separately and independently of the president. Even agencies that are not technically independent, such as the Federal Bureau of Investigation, are required to maintain independence to ensure the best interests of the people are upheld. The president of the United States should honor and uphold the very principles that preserve and protect the democratic process. Anything less is, frankly, un-American.

CONGRESS

When I first arrived on Capitol Hill as a new member of Congress in 1989, I was more than a little surprised to discover a steady stream of gifts arriving at my office. I quickly learned it was common for congressional offices to receive such largesse. The "generous benefactors" were typically businesses and organizations who had interests before the federal government, and the gifts were usually quite nice. Among the items I can recall delivered to the office were bundles of wrapping paper, expensive candies, designer perfume, and even a silver-plated salad fork and spoon set. I immediately instituted a comprehensive no-gifts policy.

After seeking appropriate legal counsel and analyzing reasonable options, my staff and I determined that it was less time-consuming and more cost-effective to give the gifts to local charities than to pack them up and send them back to the benefactors. Consequently, we passed the gifts on to philanthropic organizations, and we maintained a record of all the gifts and charities.

Over time, I decided that I needed to do more than merely not accept such gifts, because I believed that this practice of gift giving to members of Congress was wrong for the democratic process. As presented previously, it can be difficult for people, including legislators, to say no to a business or organization that gave them a gift. In July 1993, I introduced legislation, the Congressional Ethics Reform Act (H.R. 2735),[17] banning members and congressional staff from accepting gifts from anyone other than family members or personal friends. My specific bill was not passed by Congress, but a number of provisions like those in my bill were adopted in subsequent legislation.

Something else that surprised me in my first year serving in the US House was that, at that time, members of Congress had the authority to raise their own pay. In 1989, a bill to raise the salaries of members of Congress was passed and signed into law. I opposed the legislation.[18] I not only voted against the bill, but after the increase went into effect, I returned the amount of my raise to the US Treasury.

While increasing the salaries of public officials may at times be good policy, a public servant should never be able to raise his or her own salary. There is an inherent conflict between one's personal interest in having a higher income and the public's interest in paying public officials a fair and reasonable salary. I believed then, and I believe now, that there should be a requirement that any salary increase cannot take effect until after an election has been held. That way, the voters can decide if they want to rehire an elected official and pay him or her a higher salary.

James Madison also thought that members of the House and Senate should not be able to raise their own salaries, and he introduced a constitutional amendment prohibiting "varying the compensation for the services of the Senators and Representatives" until an election has "intervened." Initially to be included in the Bill of Rights, Congress submitted the text to the states on September 25, 1789. It took some time, but finally, 203 years later on May 7, 1992, it was ratified as the Twenty-Seventh Amendment by the vote of Michigan. Article II, Section 1 of the Constitution contains such a provision preventing the president's salary from being raised during the specific term for which he or she has been elected.

US senators and representatives serve as the voice of the people, and doing that well requires regular interactions with constituents. Developing personal relationships is an integral part of the job. But it also makes it difficult to be objective. I think writing a code of ethics that finds the perfect balance between relationship building and minimal conflicts of interest is probably not possible. Even so, since the time I was serving in the early 1990s, Congress has clearly made improvements in tightening ethics parameters and strengthening the ethics code.

Unlike in the executive branch, where the president and vice president are not covered by the Fourteen Principles, in the Congress, all members are covered by the ethics provisions. That doesn't mean that every member strictly follows the rules or the laws. But it does mean that there are consequences for violations.

Gifts

The restrictions on members of Congress are more stringent today than they were when I was serving in the House. Members of the US House and Senate, as well as their staffs, may not accept *any* gift from a registered lobbyist, foreign agent, or an entity that retains or employs such individuals.[19] No longer can lobbyists wine and dine senators and representatives, or take them to ball games or tennis matches, or host them for a game of golf. Neither can individuals or organizations that retain a lobbyist.

Members of the US House and Senate and their staffs may accept gifts from family members and personal friends. If a gift from a friend is valued over $250, however, members and staff must receive written approval from the House or Senate Ethics Committee, respectively, before accepting the gift. Cash, including gift cards and prepaid debit cards, may not be accepted from anyone other than a family member or personal friend.[20]

Since 1980, more than two dozen members of the House and Senate have been indicted, and the most common charge was bribery. In these cases, members were accused of accepting money in exchange for official actions helpful to the benefactor.[21] The number of members indicted is less than 1 percent of the total serving in the two bodies of Congress. But even one indictment means that someone in whom we have placed our trust has undercut the principles of democracy. The lure of a gift, especially a large one, can be overpowering for some.

While the objective of the no-gift restriction is not technically to prevent conflicts of interest, in a broad sense, it addresses that issue. We like to be nice to people who give us something of value, and it is very easy to lose objectivity when we know that our actions will impact someone who has presented us with a gift. The purpose of the gift restriction pertaining to members and staff is to minimize unfair influence in the legislative process. As such, this provision is significant to upholding democratic principles of equal participation in the governing process.

Conflicts of Interest and Exploitation

Members and staff may not use their official position or their access to nonpublic information for personal gain. Doing so puts their personal interests above the public's interests. While performing their official responsibilities, members of the House and Senate, as well as their staff, often have access to confidential information. They are prohibited from using such information in ways that could benefit them or their families.

These restrictions sound very reasonable and straightforward. But while some types of conflicts of interest are obvious and clear, others are more tenuous and less apparent.

For example, there is clearly a conflict if a member owns a parcel of land and writes or supports legislation specifically identifying that land as a location for a military installation. But other situations are a bit murky, as in the following illustration. A member of Congress who is a veteran of military service would have experience and knowledge that would be an asset to the Committee on Veterans' Affairs. But he or she may potentially be personally eligible to receive veterans' benefits being proposed in legislation considered by that very committee. A vote in favor of a veterans' program might also be a vote to benefit him or her. Could that cause a conflict of interest? Should military veterans be prohibited from serving on the House or Senate Veterans' Committee or from voting on legislation pertaining to veterans' benefits, given that a vote in favor of increasing benefits to veterans could be personally beneficial to them?

I believe that the veteran example is materially different than the example of the member benefitting from legislation that designates his or her parcel of land for development of a military installment. While the veteran may benefit from a veterans' program he or she supports, the benefit is not specific to that one individual, and it does not exclude others from the process. I also believe that veterans bring useful and important knowledge to policy-making pertaining to veterans, and the value of their input would be lost if they were prohibited from serving on the Senate or House committee responsible for public policy pertaining to veterans' issues.

JUDICIAL BRANCH

The US courts were created by our founding fathers to administer justice in a fair and impartial manner.

Ensuring fairness and impartiality in the judiciary is not an easy task. It is an undertaking that is at least as challenging for the judicial branch as it is for the other two branches of government. Courts have a duty to aspire to the highest level of fairness. For democracy to work, there must be a real, as well as a perceived, evenhandedness in the court system.

Accomplishing such fairness requires an impartial process and dedicated judges who are as unbiased as humanly possible and who have an exceedingly high level of knowledge and dedication. Article III, Section 2 of the Constitution guarantees that the trial of crimes shall be by a jury of peers, and the Sixth Amendment guarantees the right to a speedy and public trial. But like the rest of us, peers and presiding judges are human, and they also have their own beliefs, presumptions, and biases.

As in the legislative and executive branches, the judiciary has an ethics code for judges. It establishes standards of behavior for judges, and these rules cover both professional and personal behavior.

Following is the code of conduct for federal judges.

Code of Conduct for US Judges

Canon 1: A Judge Should Uphold the Integrity and Independence of the Judiciary.

Canon 2: A Judge Should Avoid Impropriety and the Appearance of Impropriety in All Activities.

Canon 3: A Judge Should Perform the Duties of the Office Fairly, Impartially and Diligently.

Canon 4: A Judge May Engage in Extrajudicial Activities That are Consistent with the Obligations of Judicial Office.

Canon 5: A Judge Should Refrain from Political Activity.[22]

Compared to the provisions in the codes of conduct for other government officials, these are quite strict. A judge is not to even appear to be improper and may only engage in extrajudicial activities that are consistent with the obligations of the office. He or she may not participate in political activities. These are all aimed at protecting the democratic principle of fairness for both process and judgment.

Historically, across the federal courts, there has been considerable disparity in how courts have ruled and sentenced. Toward the goal of reducing this inconsistency, Congress created the US Sentencing Commission, as part of the Sentencing Reform Act of 1984. The commission is an independent agency whose mission includes establishing sentencing policies and practices, advising and assisting Congress and the executive branch in developing criminal policy, and collecting and analyzing data to provide useful information as a resource for all three branches of government as well as the public.[23]

Unfortunately, inconsistencies in sentencing continue. We know, for example, that there are both racial and gender disparities in sentencing for convictions of the same offense. In federal criminal cases, on average, women receive shorter prison sentences than men,[24] and black people receive sentences that are about 10 percent longer than the sentences of white people. Equally troubling, black men are incarcerated about six times the rate at which white men are incarcerated.[25]

These findings reflect a process that is failing to uphold the democratic principle of justice. Clearly, we are not doing enough to resolve the disparities. That women get lighter sentences than men or that white people get lighter sentences than minorities reflects a failure in the execution of democratic values. Some of this disparity is likely due to a federal bench whose composition does not reflect the composition of the population it serves. In research conducted in 2016, it was found that about 60 percent of our federal judges were white men, 11 percent were black, and 7 percent were Latino. Only about one-fourth of federal judges were women.[26] And we know from research that people have unconscious biases, usually regarding people who are perceived as different from themselves.

We need a more diverse judiciary. While it would be unrealistic to expect that greater diversity on the bench will lead to perfect equity in the judicial process, there should be no doubt that there would be improvement. Our national character would be stronger. Every president has the obligation to nominate competent judges who reflect the diversity of our population. Fairness in the judicial process is central to democracy and the American character.

ETHICS AND FEDERAL ELECTIONS

In a democratic society, the process by which we adopt laws and the content of the laws themselves are both important. The same can be said of elections. How we choose our public officials is as important as the choices we make. The democratic principle of equal access to governing is as relevant to the ways in which we elect our leaders as it is to the ways in which we write and enforce our laws. For democracy to work, the electoral process must be fair and transparent, and it must safeguard the right of eligible voters to participate equally.

Campaign and election laws are broad, detailed, and complex, and entire books have been written on these topics. I believe three areas of immediate concern are campaign finance, congressional district maps, and voter suppression. To improve fairness in the political process and strengthen our democracy, we need policy reform in all three areas.

Campaign Finance

When George Washington served in the Virginia House of Burgesses, prior to becoming our nation's first president, elections were quite different than they are today. Rather than being held at regularly scheduled intervals, they were held when called by the governor. And voters would cast their votes by standing in front of a crowd and verbally stating the name of their chosen candidate.

Sometimes election days were more than a little unruly because candidates often sought the favor of voters by plying them with food and alcoholic beverages. Today, such an approach to campaigning would be illegal, because it would be considered a way of buying votes. Even George Washington provided food and drinks for the voters during at least some of his elections.[27]

The father of our country was known as a man of integrity and character.[28] Even though the story of him chopping down his father's cherry tree was a legend created by an itinerant minister and bookseller, it reflected the truth about his honesty and judgment.[29] So what might explain why he would give voters food and drink in exchange for their votes? It was probably the result of inexperience with elections and the democratic process. Our founding fathers likely had little-to-no understanding of the psychology of human behavior and the influence food and drink can have on decision-making. There had not been the time and experience needed to understand and develop the kinds of parameters needed to ensure free and fair voting.

We have come a long way since those early elections. Over the years, Congress has worked to address issues that conflict with or threaten the underlying principles of free and fair elections. There is still much work to be done, and the undertaking is not an easy one. We are all aware of ways in which political interests can conflict and interfere with good policy, including the laws that impact campaigns and elections. For example, many who have money and power would like to expand their opportunities to use their money and power to influence elections. It is not unusual for selfish interests to win over public interests.

There are also very legitimate challenges to election fairness that come from the need to protect individual rights guaranteed by our Constitution. Finding the right balance in addressing these concerns is not easy. As an example, many of us believe that money plays too great a role in the political process, and we believe that wealth or income should not determine one's ability to influence the outcome of an election. Clearly, a candidate with the means to self-fund his or her own campaign has a financial advantage over a candidate who does not have such means. This causes an imbalance in the political process. The First Amendment, however, guarantees each of us the right to speak, without the government abridging that right. And it would be wrong to deny any candidate the right of free speech, including the use of one's own money to communicate a message to the voters.

Campaign finance laws provide numerous restrictions designed to protect the integrity of our elections, as well as the rights of individual voters to fair and equal access to political participation. Among the many legal provisions and restrictions pertaining to federal elections are the following:

- For 2019–2020 federal elections, individuals may contribute a maximum of $2,800 in the primary and $2,800 in the general to a specific campaign, for a total of $5,600. This limit is indexed for inflation in odd-numbered years.
- A campaign may not accept more than $100 in cash from an individual source for a nominating campaign or election to federal office.
- The value of an in-kind contribution counts against the contribution limit and is subject to the same restrictions as a monetary contribution.
- It is illegal to contribute in someone else's name.
- Corporations, not-for-profit corporations, labor organizations, and federal government contractors are prohibited from contributing to federal campaigns.
- Foreign nationals are prohibited from contributing to federal campaigns.
- Churches, with their tax-exempt status, are prohibited from making contributions in connection with federal elections.
- Corporations, labor organizations, and other organizations may establish political action committees (PACs) that may contribute to federal campaigns. The fundraising for PACs is restricted/regulated.[30]

The purpose of these restrictions is to safeguard the political process from the imbalance of power that results from wealthy individuals and well-funded organizations disproportionately influencing the election process. The restrictions on individual contributions, for example, exist to provide a level of balance among those with different financial means. The prohibition of foreign nationals from giving to campaigns protects us from foreign interference in the electoral process that must be under the exclusive control of the governed.

While political action committees are often maligned as powerful special interests, they were originally created for the purpose of empowering individuals whose voices were often eclipsed by the voices of those who had the money and means to wield greater influence. The very first PAC was formed by the Congress of Industrial Organizations (CIO) in 1943 to support President Franklin D. Roosevelt's 1944 reelection bid.[31] By individually contributing small amounts of money to their PAC, members of the CIO were able to unify and strengthen their voices and influence. It allowed them to be heard in a political arena often dominated by personal wealth and power.

A major ruling by the US Supreme Court has fundamentally expanded the way that special interests can function and, consequently, tilted the political process further in favor of powerful interests. Specifically, the January 2010, Supreme Court ruling in the *Citizens United* case allows unlimited expenditures by corporations, unions, and other groups for campaign messages that encourage votes for or against a candidate. While there must not be coordination with the candidate's campaign, this decision has resulted in a bigger role for big money in politics and elections.[32]

As stated on the Federal Election Commission website, "Political committees that make only independent expenditures and the non-contribution accounts of Hybrid PACs may solicit and accept unlimited contributions from individuals, corporations, labor organizations and other political committees."[33]

In addition to concentrating power in the hands of a fewer number of individuals, allowing unlimited contributions also creates the potential for substantial conflicts of interest. These rulings expanded the right of free speech to corporations and other organizations. This allows the money of organizations to drown out the voices of individuals, and that undermines the principle of fairness and equal access in the political process.

In regulating unlimited individual contributions to Hybrid PACs, one of the challenges is the same as with the issue regarding the right of a candidate to spend unlimited amounts of personal money on his or her own campaign for federal office. The constitutional right to freedom of expression prohibits the federal government from restricting what people say and how they say it. But we can and should pursue a constitutional amendment that draws a distinction between the rights of expression for individuals and those of organizations, including corporations.

We must ensure complete transparency regarding unlimited financial contributions made to influence elections. We know that financial support for political campaigns influences the legislative process and therefore legislative outcomes. There needs to be further regulation regarding disclosure, because we all have a right to know who is funding political campaigns. We also need to find ways to strengthen everyone's voices by expanding opportunities for small donor participation.

Congressional District Maps

How we draw congressional district maps influences the fairness of our elections. Congressional districts are often constructed in ways that concentrate voters of one political party in a smaller number of districts than is representative of the actual number of voters in that party. This can result in one party receiving a smaller share of seats than actual votes, while the other party receives a larger share of seats than votes. With technology that allows us to quickly and easily evaluate large sets of data, it has become increasingly easy to politicize the drawing of congressional districts.

In 2016, Republican candidates running for the US House received 49.9 percent of the votes cast, while Democratic candidates received 47.3 percent of the votes cast. But Republicans won 55.2 percent, and Democrats won 44.8 percent of the seats in the House. In other words, Republicans won a "seats bonus."[34]

In 2010, 2012, and 2014, Democratic House candidates received a greater share of actual votes than the share of seats won. Additionally, in 2012, Democratic candidates won more votes in total than did Republican candidates, but Republicans won a majority of House seats.[35]

This practice is not unique to the Republican Party; Democrats have drawn the district lines to benefit their party in many states over the years. Regardless of who does it, engaging in acts that deliberately skew the results of an election clearly undercuts the democratic process.

Research conducted by the Brennan Center for Justice indicates that congressional maps adopted in states where a single party controls the process are less responsive to the actual vote totals of the electorate than in states where there is a more politically neutral process for drawing the maps.[36] These findings suggest that we need to ensure a more balanced and fair process for constructing congressional district maps. We must take the responsibility and authority for drawing these maps out of the political process by creating nonpolitical commissions to draw the congressional and state legislative maps.

New maps are drawn every ten years, after the decennial Census data have been collected and analyzed. If we truly support the democratic process, then we must insist that each state use a fair and balanced process to draw its congressional maps.

Voter Suppression

Across our country, we have seen a variety of approaches used to make it more difficult for certain voter groups to participate in our political process, which of course also undermines democracy. Among these methods are restrictive voter identification laws, reductions in early voting opportunities, and rules that make voter registration more difficult, including aggressive purging of voters from registration files. In the time period following the 2010 elections through May 2019, twenty-five states adopted new restrictions.[37]

Those who support such tactics argue that there is widespread voter fraud. But research shows that voter fraud, defined as "intentional corruption of the electoral process by the voter" is extremely rare.[38] Rather, "most voter fraud allegations turn out to be something other than fraud" . . . and "there is a long history in America of elites using voter fraud allegations to restrict and shape the electorate" and "the historically disenfranchised are often the target of voter fraud allegations."[39]

It is clearly wrong to deny other people the right to something that is legitimately theirs. Engaging in voter suppression chips away at the very foundation of our country. As President John F. Kennedy said in his report to the American People on Civil Rights, "the rights of every man are diminished when the rights of one man are threatened."[40]

We must recognize voter suppression tactics for what they are. Even more, we must stand up to those who use such tactics to expand their own power at the expense of fellow citizens and the democratic process.

FIVE

DEMOCRACY, ETHICS, AND CAPITALISM

The first truth is that the liberty of a democracy is not safe if the people tolerate the growth of private power to a point where it becomes stronger than their democratic state itself. . . . The second truth is that the liberty of a democracy is not safe, if its business system does not provide employment and produce and distribute goods in such a way as to sustain an acceptable standard of living.

PRESIDENT FRANKLIN D. ROOSEVELT[1]

MACROETHICS IN BUSINESS

The role of corporate social responsibility is more than a mere topic for academic debate. I believe it has relevance to long-term economic performance, and when I first read these words of President Franklin D. Roosevelt, I could not help but think about Milton Friedman's famous essay titled "The Social Responsibility of Business Is to Increase Its Profits," published in the *New York Times Magazine* on September 13, 1970.[2] That fall I was a college freshman at Valparaiso University, and I remember very well my generation's political activism, which included pushing the corporate sector to be more socially engaged and accountable.

A couple years later, I was introduced to this essay in a business economics class and can vaguely recall not being convinced that his analysis was very sound. That may suggest a bit of youthful arrogance on my part. Dr. Friedman was a brilliant and prolific economist whose work earned him the international honor of the Nobel Prize in Economic Sciences just a few years later in 1976. To this day, I still find his analysis very thought provoking, but I continue to question his conclusion.

Being part of a society means that we have responsibilities to that society. I believed then and continue to believe that businesses of any size or structure—proprietorships, partnerships, or corporations whose shares are privately owned or publicly traded—have social responsibility that is broader than their specific function. In a democratic society with a capitalist economy, we are given freedoms, rights, and opportunities, and we all have the responsibility to protect those freedoms, rights, and opportunities. Corporate social responsibility that extends beyond profitable operations is a necessity, because business does not operate in a vacuum and most, if not all, business decisions impact society in some way. Every individual and organization, including for-profit enterprises, has an obligation to the society of which we are a part.

The strategic process for ethical decision-making presented in chapter 3 includes a step for analyzing how a decision will impact stakeholders. For capitalism to thrive, business decisions must reflect the larger interests of the people who are a part of the economy. This is a basic responsibility of business; long-term economic health depends on the economic strength of the people who are a part of the economy.

If the for-profit sector is not socially responsible, over time there will be costs to society, some of which will erode the purchasing power of customers, including ultimate consumers. That will impact the larger economy and profit potential for individual firms. Research on this topic has suggested that corporate social responsibility contributes positively to a nation's competitiveness and standard of living.[3]

In the half century since Dr. Friedman's paper was published, many economists and other social scientists have debated his assertion. I think debating his essay still has relevance. It would appear that others also see its pertinence to the modern economy, as the discussion continues. Recently the Brookings Institution, as part of their Center for Effective Public Management's Initiative on Twenty-First Century Capitalism, published a paper in which its authors argue that the corporate sector is viewed differently by the public today than in 1970 and that there exists a market-based belief in the responsibility of business to maximize value for society.[4]

This market-based belief in corporate social responsibility seems to be the opposite of Dr. Friedman's stance, but maybe the two positions are not completely inconsistent with one another. In his essay, he wrote, "In a free-enterprise, private-property system, a corporate executive is an employee of the owners of the business. He has direct responsibility to his employers. That responsibility is to conduct the business in accordance with their desires, which generally will be to make as much money as possible while conforming to the basic rules of the society, both those embodied in law and those embodied in ethical custom."[5]

If a society's values include the belief or an expectation on the part of customers that corporations have a responsibility to contribute to the good of the broader society, then executive management would be advised to conduct business in a way that reflects that. Corporate social responsibility is a macroethics issue, and if ethical customs include accountability for the long-term best interest of the community, a corporation's actions should reflect that. More basically, if social accountability helps strengthen the economy, then it will potentially lead to greater opportunity for long-term profitability.

Over the years, economists and other social scientists have conducted research to determine if corporate social responsibility correlates with profitability or stock value. There has been considerable variation in how the studies have been conducted, and the findings have been mixed. While some researchers have found a positive correlation, others have found no correlation, and still others have found a negative correlation.

We know that a business's short-term and long-term financial performance is the result of many factors, not all of them within the control of executive management. Obviously, profitability and strong stock value depend on sound strategic planning and implementation, combined with favorable macroeconomic conditions. I can think of no theory in the field of economics that would suggest that long-term financial success and corporate social responsibility are mutually exclusive.

Consistent with my belief are research findings published by the Federal Reserve Bank of St. Louis. The authors found that recent analyses, both empirical and theoretical, show companies can strategically engage in socially responsible activities that lead to increased profits. Specifically, they determined that social efforts that enhance the company's reputation and differentiate its products and that help attract more highly qualified personnel can translate into greater profitability.[6]

This analysis supports the argument for strategic corporate social responsibility, but it does not suggest any specific approach to doing so. Nor does it suggest that such responsibility is an obligation of the business sector. The point is not that businesses should use their resources to randomly support projects that just happen to have social value. It would not make sense, for example, for every business to support the arts or build a local park for the community. But as members of a capitalist economy, all businesses have a responsibility to recognize the long-term social impact of their operations.

How they conduct business affects the strength of the social fabric, and that impacts the economy. This is not just a moral, feel-good approach to corporate leadership; it shows an understanding of a relationship between social responsibility, the larger macroeconomy, and the potential for profitability of an individual business.

Any discussion of corporate social responsibility would be incomplete without at least a mention of the social value of capitalism. Although capitalism is an economic structure often maligned by politicians and social activists, its long-term success clearly shows that it is the economic model that is most effective in building and sustaining wealth and resources for a society.

At least since the middle of the twentieth century, capitalism has outperformed other economic structures and, therefore, has demonstrated the greatest potential for supporting social value to the people. From 1950 to 2015, the average per-capita gross domestic product generated in the advanced capitalist economies was consistently multiple times greater than the average per-capita gross domestic product generated by other economies.[7] In other words, capitalist economies have produced and sold more products and have been more economically successful than other types of economies.

Given that protecting, sheltering, feeding, clothing, and educating a population depend on a country's economic strength, one can reasonably argue that social responsibility is not possible without a consistently strong economy. Additionally, a democratic government that is well run and that protects the rights of the individual requires financial resources to develop and adopt, as well as execute, effective policy. For me, capitalism as a mere concept is socially responsible; it provides us the greatest potential for developing the economic means necessary for serving our people and for being socially responsible.

I am also confident in my belief that solid ethical principles are at the very heart of capitalism. Central to this economic structure is the right of private ownership, and that shows respect for the individual, which is a universally accepted pillar of ethics. The freedoms to choose a career in business and to pursue new ideas and inventions are often taken for granted here in the United States. But these freedoms are reflective of a liberating ideology. A private sector market open to individuals provides us freedom to make our own choices. Is that not a liberal concept?

Per capita economic achievement and growth, and liberating principles, are only part of the equation, however, because freedoms are not free. With capitalistic opportunities come obligations to society. A major obligation of businesses is to pay fair wages to their employees. A full-time worker should not have to live in poverty.

For a country to be strong, there must be equity and balance in the distribution of its economic resources and wealth. Just as we in the United States have been far from perfect in running our democracy, we have been far from perfect in running our businesses. And our public policy that impacts business and workers has also been far from perfect.

These are complex issues, but we must always remember that America's character is based on providing freedoms and opportunities that make it possible for individuals to pursue their interests and realize their potential.

In the debate pertaining to the laws that impact businesses and workers, some people advocate for completely free, unregulated business enterprise. Their basic argument is that innovation and hard work will be rewarded and that people will be motivated by the rewards for working hard. This will lead to growth in the economy.

If someone chooses not to work, he or she will eventually realize that work is necessary to survival, and that realization will motivate him or her to get a job or start a business. After all, in a market economy, business owners are not the only ones who have responsibilities. Employees have obligations, too, including the duty to come to work ready and willing to provide an honest day's work for an honest day's pay.

It is true that business owners and employees both share the responsibility of making capitalism succeed. It is also true that rewards often come to those who are innovative and who work hard. Completely free markets do not work perfectly, however, and there are often extenuating circumstances that make it difficult for individuals to find employment or stay employed.

On the other side of the business regulation issue are those who favor a very heavy-handed approach on the part of the government. They would argue, for example, that income inequality can be reduced by setting financial limits on corporate executive compensation.

I believe that our greatest potential for continued economic and social strength will come from a policy approach that lies between these two outer limits. For us to be our best, there must be reasonable laws and regulations that protect the market economy while simultaneously safeguarding businesses and people from the uncertainties of market-driven commerce. But we must avoid overregulation that stifles innovation, growth, and profitability.

I personally like a combination of carrots and sticks. Tax incentives that make it financially feasible for businesses to provide retirement plans to their employees are an example of a carrot that has had a strong and positive macroeffect on our economy. An example of a stick that has been advantageous to consumers and the larger economy would be airline safety regulations. Confidence in the safety of air travel has been integral to the growth and profitability of the industry, and good for the overall economy.

Finding the right combination of carrots and sticks to preserve our market economy and help it thrive is a never-ending challenge. Data collection and analysis are important to the development and adoption of good public policy. Adding to the challenge are the competing political interests, but it is an infinitely important task to ensuring economic balance.

And the importance of economic balance and social equity to economic strength cannot be overemphasized. Few would argue that our long-term economic and social strength are dependent on broad access to economic opportunity. Nor would they argue that economic disenfranchisement undermines and erodes that strength. Fair compensation for employees is only one of the variables important to our economic and social strength. The opportunity for quality education is also important.

Today there is serious cause for concern in the United States. Income inequality has grown considerably over the last several decades, and the result is a weakened economic structure.

A common measure of income inequality is the Gini index, which was developed in 1912 by the Italian statistician Corrado Gini. The Gini coefficient measures actual income distribution against a perfectly equal income distribution; a higher coefficient reflects greater income inequality. If everyone had equal wealth, the coefficient would be 0; if only one person held all the wealth, the coefficient would be 100.[8] According to an analysis of data conducted by the Federal Reserve Bank of St. Louis, between 1979 and 2016, the coefficient grew from 34.6 to 41.5.[9]

The issue of wealth concentration is not just a matter of ethical concern. How income and wealth are distributed among a population also impacts the overall strength of a country. Results of recent research "show clear evidence that in the United States wide-ranging inequality substantially lowers people's trust in each other" as well as their trust in government.[10] There exists a large body of literature revealing that social cohesion and economic growth are impacted by the level of trust people have in others and in institutions.

For example, with lowered trust among private sector institutions, insurance and legal costs go up, and therefore, cost efficiency is reduced. In the public sector, lack of trust makes it more difficult for those who have differing opinions to find common solutions.[11] Public trust steadily declined during that same time period.

Clearly, income inequality is an issue that must be addressed, and for at least a century, labor unions have demonstrated considerable effectiveness in addressing this issue. Over the years, many studies have been conducted on the impacts of unionization and have shown a positive correlation between union membership and higher wages and benefits. In one recent study, researchers at Princeton and Columbia Universities conducted several comprehensive analyses on labor unions and income inequality, using data from 1936 forward. Their findings provide evidence that unions have played a significant role in reducing income inequality.[12]

Those who oppose unionized labor often argue that unions drive up the cost of labor to the detriment of the firm's profitability. The same could be said of higher executive salaries. Between 1978 and 2017, CEO compensation, including stock options, rose by 979 percent while the stock market (S&P Index) grew at a much lower rate of 637 percent. In 2017, the average CEO salary in the 350 largest firms in the United States was almost $19 million. Additionally, the 2017 CEO-to-worker compensation ratio was 312 to 1, compared to a ratio of 58 to 1 in 1989.[13] In other research studying the effect of unionization during 1983–1999, it was found that there was little or no effect on business dislocation.[14]

These research findings indicate that this issue reaches beyond the matters of macroethics and social responsibility. Equity and stability in incomes are important to a nation's success. This should make it very clear that there exists a need for reasonable regulations and enforcement pertaining to the labor force in a capitalist economy. Societies are stronger when people have confidence that businesses are being run fairly. Just as people must be accountable to one another, businesses must be accountable to the people. Accountability and integrity are ethical pillars that make clear the importance of corporate social responsibility to American character.

MICROETHICS IN BUSINESS

Macroethics concerns are only part of the equation for ensuring that business contributes to, and doesn't detract from, America's character. Just as microethics decisions in government can have broad impact on our overall national strength, microethics decisions in business can have broad impact on our overall economic strength. The Great Recession that began in December 2007 was the result of a meltdown in the financial services and housing sectors brought about, in part, by unethical behavior of many individuals working in the fields of finance and banking.

As stated earlier, business success is determined by the combination of strategic management decisions and occurrences in the broader macroeconomic environment. While executives do not have control over the larger environment in which their businesses function, they do have control over how their respective firms are managed. They determine the ethical culture of their organization. Running a business in an ethical way is more significant to the bottom line than many people realize.

Economists at the Federal Reserve Bank of Boston conducted research in which they studied the impact of financial losses on a firm's overall value. Specifically, they compared changes in stock prices for firms who experienced financial losses due to fraud to those firms who experienced financial losses due to external events beyond their control. They found that "market values fall one-for-one with losses caused by external events, but fall by over twice the loss percentage in cases involving internal fraud."[15] A correlation does not establish cause and effect, but these findings certainly indicate that engaging in fraudulent activity can be twice as costly as making an honest strategic mistake.

I think the findings in this research also help explain the magnitude of the Great Recession. As financial institutions experienced losses due to a lack of integrity regarding microethics matters in their operations, the value of their firms eroded beyond the value of the actual losses. The combination of the loss in trust and the loss of money caused the situation to snowball.

Reasonable people can disagree, and there are many who disagree with my belief in the need for regulations. I understand why someone would want to run a business without government restraint. But that simply does not work. While it is common for us to think that we don't need regulations to run a business well, most of us believe that others should be restrained. And we expect them to follow rules for ensuring greater order and fairness in society.

As presented in chapter 2, most people do not progress beyond the conventional stage of moral development. In that stage, they believe it is important to have rules because doing so creates social order. But most people do not give the rules a great deal of thought, and they do not recognize the intrinsic value of virtues and principles. And some people do not even develop past the preconventional state.

Generally speaking, however, most people believe that rules and laws are necessary. A review of deregulation of the financial services sector in the late twentieth and early twenty-first centuries may provide some insight. In the twenty-five years leading up to the financial meltdown, our federal government took numerous deregulatory actions. In other words, the laws affecting the operations of financial institutions were weakened.

For example, in 1980, the Regulation Q ceilings on deposit interest rates were abolished, and that allowed banks to compete more aggressively. Then in 1982, Congress deregulated the savings and loan industry, allowing it to enter into new areas of lending. In 1986, the Federal Reserve began allowing commercial banks to generate up to 5 percent of their income from investment banking activities. And in 1999, the passage of Gramm-Leach-Bliley allowed institutions to combine commercial banking, investment banking, and insurance underwriting, essentially removing all remaining Glass-Steagall restrictions adopted following the Great Depression.[16]

Recent research at the International Monetary Fund suggests that the regulatory environment is a factor in financial crises. Specifically, a study of the "political economy of financial policy during ten of the most infamous financial booms and busts since the 18th century" found "financial booms, and risk-taking during these episodes, were often amplified by political regulatory stimuli, credit subsidies, and an increasing light-touch approach to financial supervision."[17]

Warren Buffett said, "Honesty is a very expensive gift—don't expect it from cheap people."[18] The fact is that most of us need rules establishing behavioral boundaries that are good for the greater society. We behave better when we have rules and enforcement. But more importantly, for American character to survive, we need rules. A well-thought-out regulatory system built upon legitimate research findings from the field of economics helps us to simultaneously grow our economy and strengthen our social fabric.

Most well-run companies have formal codes of ethics. To be effective, a code must be based on a value system that is communicated and understood throughout the organization. It must be followed and enforced by those who hold senior leadership positions, as well as by others in the company. In other words, to effectively build an ethical culture, executive leaders must make doing so a priority. Many professional associations also adopt codes of ethics for their members.

The research findings make it clear that ethics codes are necessary to ensuring the integrity of a firm's operations. Over the years, our country has been witness to many corporate scandals, many of which have caused damage to our economy. Corrupt corporate behavior, even though it occurs quite often, is not consistent with American character. With the goal of reducing such corruption and the damage it does to our economy, Congress has often responded by adopting laws that increase regulatory oversight.

As an outcome of these laws, there now exist numerous regulations requiring businesses to adopt governance policies that include formal ethics codes. For example, the Federal Deposit Insurance Corporation (FDIC) has issued a guidance letter pertaining to corporate codes of conduct for this sector of the economy. Following is a summary of its provisions.

Summary of FDIC Guidance on Implementing an Effective Ethics Program

An institution's board of directors should convey the message that integrity and ethical values of the highest standard should be maintained. The board should establish clear expectations on acceptable business practices and prohibited conflicts of interest by establishing policies on expected behavior. Management should ensure that these policies are communicated and understood throughout the organization. Issues that should be addressed in these policies include:

Safeguarding Confidential Information

Ensuring the Integrity of Records

Providing Strong Internal Controls Over Assets

Providing Candor in Dealing with Auditors, Examiners and
    Legal Counsel

Avoiding Self-dealings and Acceptance of Gifts or Favors

An institution's corporate code of conduct or ethics policy should prohibit any employee, officer, director, agent or attorney of any bank from:

1. Soliciting for themselves or for a third party anything of value from anyone in return for any business, service or confidential information of the bank, and

2. Accepting anything of value from anyone in connection with the business of the bank, either before or after a transaction is discussed or consummated.

The board of directors should ensure that bank management is cognizant of all applicable laws and regulations. Further, the board should make certain that compliance with all laws and regulations receives a high priority and that violations are not knowingly committed by bank employees.[19]

The FDIC insures up to $250,000 for each depositor in an insured institution, and the insurance fund is backed by the full faith and credit of the US government.[20] In other words, if there are a large number of bank failures and the fund is unable to cover the insured accounts, the federal government will cover the shortfall. Since Congress created the FDIC in 1933, during the Great Depression, no depositor has lost even a penny in an insured fund.[21]

This guidance letter demonstrates an understanding of the relationship between ethical management and the health of the broader economy. As would be expected, its provisions are consistent with the six pillars of character. Safeguarding confidential information is a demonstration of responsibility and trustworthiness. Ensuring the integrity of records, providing candor in professional dealings, and avoiding self-dealings and acceptance of gifts or favors all reflect integrity.

These are all important to the long-term well-being of individual institutions and are equally important to a strong financial services sector. And more generally, ethics are important to the health of our overall economy.

Since the Great Depression, the US economy has experienced a number of recessions. Economic downturns are generally caused by a number of factors, including "natural" and predictable corrections in the economy. But unethical behavior in the public and private sectors has also been a causal factor in some economic downturns. For example, politics playing too great a role in monetary and fiscal policy contributed to the Great Depression. The Great Recession was the result of the subprime mortgage crisis, and the recession of 1990–1991 was largely the result of the savings and loan crisis.

Too often, business and public policy decisions are based on successful lobbying by interest groups rather than on facts. The results can be quite costly.

In a democracy with a capitalist economy, we all have a role to play. Broad and consistent violations of microethics principles have negative macro impacts. If we fail to recognize the social responsibilities that come with self-government and a market economy, there will also be negative macro effects.

In chapter 2, I mentioned Jim Collins's research on highly successful companies. He discovered that the most effective chief executive officers, whom he labeled Level 5 leaders, consistently demonstrated character and ethics in their leadership. They demonstrated American character in the way they ran their companies.

One of those corporate leaders was the late Darwin Smith. He grew up in the northeast Indiana district I represented in Congress and became a highly successful chief executive officer of Kimberly-Clark. The way he led this paper business and his life added strength to his company, his community, and his country. Following are excerpts from a brief biography published in 2004 by the Paper International Hall of Fame.

> With beginnings as an Indiana farm boy, Darwin E. Smith rose to great prominence in the paper industry and business world as chairman and chief executive officer of Kimberly-Clark Corporation. Mr. Smith was born on April 16, 1926 in Garrett, Indiana. Having served his country in World War II, he returned to the United States and attended Indiana University and Harvard Law School and graduated from both institutions with distinction...
>
> Mr. Smith is credited with turning what was perceived as a stodgy old paper company into an innovative consumer products powerhouse. As noted in a Harvard Business Review article, Kimberly-Clark is one of eleven companies on the Fortune 500 since 1965 that has been elevated from good to great and has maintained its transformed status. Mr. Smith was recognized for making this accomplishment possible...
>
> Mr. Smith also established approaches to strengthen Kimberly-Clark's people: forming the Educational Opportunities Plan to provide continuing education to all workers, and the Health Management Program to improve physical and mental health. He also worked to increase diversity among the workforce.
>
> During Mr. Smith's tenure as chairman and chief executive officer, Kimberly-Clark stockholders experienced returns of 19.6% annually, generating cumulative stock returns that were 4.1 times greater than those of the general market and outperforming venerable companies including industry rivals. It had been a welcomed change from the 20 years prior when Kimberly-Clark had fallen 36% behind the general market.
>
> His ethics and personal integrity were further exemplified away from Kimberly-Clark. He served as director of both King Ranch and The Texan Research League, and was on the National Executive Board of the Boy Scouts of America.
>
> Mr. Smith was the type of leader who gave credit for success to the employees, the managers, his predecessors, and the customers.[22]

Like many highly successful individuals, he was not a celebrity, but he knew how to honestly and fairly get the job done.

Reflecting back on Dr. Milton Friedman's essay, I wonder now if I did not fully understand what he was saying when I first read his essay those many years ago. Maybe his thinking reflected a depth and breadth I did not fully recognize. A smart business executive knows it will be easier to make a profit when there is social trust in the macroeconomic environment the company operates in and when the company is "conforming to the basic rules of the society, both those embodied in law and those embodied in ethical custom."[23]

I cannot think of a better argument for capitalism operating in a fair and well-designed regulatory environment that promotes social responsibility. It is only reasonable to believe that ethics and social responsibility are necessary for long-term economic strength and that they are in a business's financial best interest.

More significantly, for the United States to be a world leader in advancing democracy and economic opportunity, we need a strong economy. In the long run, that is most achievable through ethical commerce that protects and strengthens our capitalist economy.

SIX

—⁓—

THE AMERICAN'S CHARACTER

A community is democratic only when the humblest and weakest person can enjoy the highest civil, economic, and social rights that the biggest and most powerful possess.

A. PHILIP RANDOLPH[1]

THESE WORDS OF A. PHILIP Randolph are very poignant for me. Just as my upbringing was influenced by the World War II and Korean War veterans who lived in my home community, it was also influenced by the civil rights movement and the Vietnam War. I was an adolescent and teenager in the 1960s, and many of the stories covered on the nightly newscasts during that era were quite disturbing. It was as confusing as it was horrifying to watch news footage of young men and women being beaten and jailed for peacefully protesting racial segregation and of young soldiers fighting in a far-off war run by politicians whose words and motives we questioned.

I looked up to those young men and women as I had looked up to the veterans from my parents' generation, but there were two significant differences. These activists and soldiers were just a few years ahead of me in age, and I was watching them in real time. That experience greatly impacted my developing view of the United States and the world.

My parents and teachers taught me that living in a democracy meant we could trust our government to be open and fair and that we all shared equal rights. But what I saw on the evening news told me something different. How appalling it was to watch what was happening in my country. What kind of person would beat up another citizen for peacefully defending the rights that are promised to us all? Even more fundamentally, why would some Americans want to deny these rights to other Americans? This awful behavior made no sense to me.

At that time, I was not yet familiar with the many Jim Crow laws that were established in the South during the century following the Civil War and ratification of the Thirteenth and Fifteenth Amendments.[2] Learning of these statutes and ordinances, whose explicit purpose was to separate the races and to deny rights to those who were born with a darker skin color, was enormously disillusioning. And how distressing it is to realize that some Americans support such policies even now.

Coming of age when the nation was deeply divided over our involvement in the Vietnam War also greatly impacted my perceptions of America, its leadership, and its people. I very much wanted to believe that our political leaders were telling us the truth and that the anti-war protesters were wrong. But by the time I had completed my freshman year of college, critical content of the Pentagon Papers was being leaked to the press, confirming the very criticisms the protesters were raising regarding our involvement in the war. We learned that administrations from President Harry S. Truman to President Lyndon B. Johnson had knowingly deceived us on our engagement in Vietnam.[3]

The Pentagon Papers' revelations were awful, in and of themselves. But we also knew that countless returning soldiers were being mistreated. After arriving home, many of our veterans had difficulty finding employment, and our nation was not providing the services they needed to integrate back into a healthy and normal civilian life.[4]

Those young men and women who served during the Vietnam War and who fought for civil rights here at home were courageous Americans. They believed in the principles of democracy and were willing to risk their own lives to improve and protect the lives of others. These Americans trusted in something they deemed bigger than themselves—a free society that protects the rights of individuals. Their actions demonstrated a belief and commitment to the words written in our Declaration of Independence and Constitution. They epitomized American character.

They were young and should have been able to place their trust in our leaders. Instead, they found themselves fighting forces that were the antithesis of American character. The country we had been taught to love and respect was not doing right by them.

Growing up in the United States at that time had its challenges and difficulties, but the overall experience was also enlightening and instructive. It was then that I began to understand what it means to live in a democratic society and I also began to identify a connection between ethics and democracy.

Watching our nation's leaders, I could see that many were making decisions they believed to be the most politically expedient. Elected officials may have been calling the shots, but they were doing what they thought was desired by and acceptable to the voters who put them in public office. It is a fact that there was great unrest at that time, and many of us were skeptical of the direction in which our leaders were taking us. It is also a fact that many in our country agreed with the policy to escalate our involvement in the Vietnam War, and many also supported the enforcement of laws that segregated us.

During those formative years, I began to understand how our leaders' actions reflected the beliefs and values of the people who had voted them into office. The workings of democracy came into focus for me as I realized that our nation is only as great as the choices and actions of the citizenry. It is not just our leaders who determine how good and strong we will be as a society. Ultimately, it is all of us—we the people—who make that determination.

Civil rights and labor leader A. Philip Randolph was right when he very eloquently stated that democracy exists only when the weakest among us enjoy the same civil, economic, and social rights as the most powerful among us. I would also add that democracy can succeed merely to the extent the citizenry upholds the responsibilities that are integral to self-governance. It is not enough for leaders to understand and lead ethical lives; we all must do so.

If we believe in our country and want it to succeed, then we have a duty to protect the tenets of democracy. We must be relentless in our commitment to defend and strengthen the democratic principles that protect these basic rights that A. Philip Randolph and many others dedicated their lives to protecting. We have a duty to accept these responsibilities, not just for ourselves but also for our fellow men and women, and for the republic itself.

Understanding our civic responsibility is central to the individual American's character.

THE PEOPLE'S ETHICS

Abraham Lincoln said, "Nearly all men can stand adversity, but if you want to test a man's character, give him power."[5] In democracy, power lies with the people, and I think it could be effectively argued that many people who are dissatisfied with our country's political leadership do not fully appreciate their own power and responsibility in making the democratic process work. For any person who possesses the good fortune to hold citizenship in the United States of America, his or her character is regularly tested by the power our country gives us as citizens.

Self-governance demands a solemn commitment on the part of its people. We all have a role to play in safeguarding and strengthening our country's character, and if we are not discerning in how we use this power, we are ducking our responsibility. When we shirk our responsibilities as members of a democratic society, we are also undermining our rights and freedoms.

Living in a democracy means being a caretaker of democracy. The success of our country is determined by us, and we are all charged with the responsibility of making and keeping it strong. We have an obligation to protect the individual rights and freedoms bestowed upon us and our fellow citizens.

The equation is unambiguous: the character we have as a nation is the sum of the character we have as individuals. Democracy is a shared responsibility, and we must look inward to ourselves, as well as outward to our leaders and fellow citizens, to make it work. We must all commit to using this democratic power in a consistently responsible way. Each of us has the obligation to understand the role we play,: one of dedication to a life of purpose, integrity, honor, and personal accountability.

It is not just unethical political leaders who have the power to undercut and even destroy a democratic society. The citizenry has extraordinary power, and we have the same obligation as public officials to be ethical, to live our lives with character, and to take seriously our responsibilities of civic engagement. We are all in this together.

Every day in our country, we see people abusing the power of democracy and capitalism, and in the process, they are chipping away at our republic and oftentimes our economy. But we also see countless examples of people using these powers of democracy and capitalism in ways that epitomize integrity and character, and they strengthen our society.

The phrase *abuse of power* is quite regularly used to describe political leaders exploiting their public positions to benefit themselves and their cronies. This term is not typically invoked to describe actions of the citizenry, but in fact, individual citizens regularly abuse the democratic power they are given. For a democracy to survive, the citizenry, as well as the leadership, must demonstrate patriotism and responsibility in their own individual actions.

The lifeblood of a strong and enduring democratic society is a citizenry of good character.

PATRIOTISM AND CHARACTER

I believe that most Americans, irrespective of political affiliation, are sincere and genuine in their aspirations to be loyal and patriotic citizens. No one person or political party has a monopoly on patriotism or good policy ideas. Individuals with opposing ideologies can be equally loyal to our country, even as they disagree and argue over broad policy direction or specific policy details.

But true patriotism demands more than aspirations and loyalty. It also requires an understanding of ethics and the integral role we all have in upholding our individual duties as members of a democratic society. The privileges that come with a participatory government bring with them an obligation on the part of every person to make choices that are consistent with the values of our democracy. The benefits of living in a democratic society demand an earnestness of effort pertaining to the matters of governing.

While it is common practice for organizations to adopt formal codes of ethics, it is not common for individuals to do so. Given the significant role that citizens play in running a democracy, I believe a strong argument can be made for encouraging Americans to adopt a thoughtful, well-based personal code of ethics. While we each have the right to our own individual values and beliefs, we collectively share the responsibility of making democracy work, and that demands a serious commitment by all of us.

Patriotic Americans understand that we must commit ourselves every day to making decisions that reflect the values embodied in our Constitution. From my years in public service and higher education, including the advancing and teaching of professional ethics, I have come to believe that the widely accepted pillars of character are integral to who we are and whom we aspire to be as a nation. It is not mere coincidence that the principles of democracy are consistent with these pillars.

The values of trustworthiness, respect, responsibility, fairness, caring, and citizenship form the foundation of this great experiment we call the United States of America. They are also the essence of American patriotism and should be included in the foundation of our individual codes of ethics.

Trustworthiness

Trustworthiness demands transparency from our political leaders, and that means we must require the president and vice president to be held to the same standards of accountability as other employees of the federal government. The law that allows the holders of these two offices to be exempted from 18 U.S.C.,

Section 208 must be changed. This criminal statute should be amended to require that the president and vice president be disqualified from participating in any official governmental matter in which they have a personal financial interest that conflicts with their conscientious performance of duty.

More broadly, we must also demand honesty from political leaders. Our national character and the role we play on the world stage demand that we be a nation of people, both leaders and citizenry, who are trusted. It is difficult for us to be a world leader or to be taken seriously when a president tells, on average, fifteen untruths a day. Such behavior not only erodes our character; it also undermines our strength. As an example, when our president made an obviously false statement while addressing the United Nations on September 25, 2018, the audience responded by laughing.[6] When world leaders ridicule our president, it means that we have lost respect and standing as a nation. A country that does not have the trust and respect of its allies loses its effectiveness on the international stage.

We know that it is not uncommon for public officials to misrepresent the truth. Even public officials who have the highest integrity will occasionally misstate a fact. Most certainly, every one of us can all recall both Democrats and Republicans making questionable or erroneous statements, some more frequently than others.

The blame for any public official's mendacity does not rest solely on his or her shoulders, however, because the person who sits in elective office serves at the pleasure of the voters. Those who support untrustworthy candidates and public officials share the responsibility for all the untruths and the damage they cause.

The act of deliberately telling a lie is a microethical violation, but it has broad and long-term macroethical consequences that threaten democracy. When a public official intentionally misleads the citizenry about government policy, that person muddies the discussion and debate, interfering with the public's ability to be accurately and adequately informed.

These untruths not only mislead the American public; they also lead us to adopt laws and policies that are not in the best interest of our country and its people. A good illustration is the deception during the debate and passage of the Tax Cuts and Jobs Act of 2017. It was sold to the public using the argument that tax cuts would generate enough economic growth to cover the revenue losses incurred due to the cuts. But the tax law changes led to an increased deficit in 2019. Even more worrisome, projections show that by 2027, the combination of the Tax Cuts and Jobs Act of 2017 and the Bipartisan Budget Act of 2018 will increase our total debt by $2.4 trillion.[7] Good decision-making depends on an honest analysis of facts.

I also believe that dishonesty weakens us as a nation because when political leaders lack candor, the public loses trust in the government and in our democratic process. Trust is critical to the successful running of a democracy. We must demand truthfulness from our leaders, not just because we should hold them to a high ethical standard but also because anything less undermines our strength. Integrity is more than an ethical concept or a characteristic of a virtuous person; it is critical to the very survival of a democratic society.

The person who does not stand up to political leaders who lie is an accomplice in their deceit. Not only are accomplices in deceit no worthier of our trust than the perpetrator of the deception, but they also share in the responsibility for damage caused by that deceit. Accepting the lies of political leaders is the antithesis of patriotism.

True patriots are truthful and demand truth from their leaders.

Respect

One of the most insidious forms of disrespect is voter suppression. While often framed by advocates as necessary to prevent fraud in the election process, many restrictive election laws have been enacted for the purposes of limiting legitimate voter participation and shaping the electorate to match their political ideology.[8] Such actions undermine the rights of fellow citizens and, therefore, the principles of democracy.

Voter suppression can be found in a variety of forms, including but not limited to complicated voter registration requirements, aggressive voter purging from the voting rolls, unreasonable voter identification requirements, limited early voting opportunities, and reduced polling locations. We must demand that Congress and state legislatures address these practices that undercut citizens' rights and the democratic process.

I was two weeks shy of turning nineteen on July 1, 1971, when the Twenty-Sixth Amendment granting eighteen-year-olds the right to vote was ratified. This amendment had special meaning for my generation because so many young people between the ages of eighteen and twenty-one served in the armed forces and were willing to give their lives for our country, but were without the right to vote. The Senate report accompanying the amendment explained that most people of this age had completed high school, were mature enough to vote, and had the responsibilities of adulthood.[9]

The late Honorable Birch Bayh, my US senator at that time, authored the amendment, and his leadership on this issue reflected respect for young Americans. He also authored Title IX of the Education Amendments of 1972 prohibiting discrimination based on sex in any federally funded education program or activity. I have always seen this provision as a confirmation of the meaningful role women play in society when given the opportunity to participate and compete. The late senator's work exemplified respect.

Most of my life has been spent living in politically and socially conservative communities. As a Democrat serving in the US House of Representatives, I represented one of the most Republican congressional districts in the country. Many constituents told me that they supported me because they believed I listened to others who held viewpoints different from my own and I worked in a nonpartisan way to best serve the interests of my district.

It has long been my belief that most policy issues are complex and many-sided; the best ideas come from heterogeneous groups comprised of individuals who embrace varying ideologies and opinions. We make better decisions when we understand others' experiences and perspectives and when we respect the merits of opposing points of view. It is important to recognize that not one of us has all the answers. We can learn from others with whom we disagree, and respect for others creates value.

Disagreement, debate, and discussion can be very useful to the democratic process; they can help us look more broadly and deeply as we seek solutions for addressing our challenges. We must never confuse disagreement and debate with stubborn antagonism, however. A mulish unwillingness to compromise on matters of public policy, in most circumstances, is not patriotic. While one should never yield in ways that violate or sacrifice the democratic principles encompassed in our Constitution, government by the people demands cooperation and compromise.

The United States is currently experiencing political divisions as deep as I have seen in my lifetime. Far too many of our people are unwilling to listen to opposing points of view or seek common areas of agreement. There are people in both major parties, as well as in smaller political parties and movements, who embody such obstinacy. While we have a right for our voices to be heard and incorporated into policy-making, none of us has a right to insist that "my way is the right way and no other way will do."

In a democracy, government is by "the people," not "by the person," and none of us should expect to have the power of a dictator or an autocrat.

Since no one person is a nation, no one person gets his or her own individual representative, senator, or president. By design, we share public officials with the rest of the population, and it is undemocratic for any one of us to expect or demand an elected official to be perfectly aligned with our own individual beliefs. Reasonableness is a necessary component of successful democratic governance.

If we want our democracy to survive, then we must accept and even embrace the value of compromise. We must recognize that people who come from different backgrounds and experiences have different perspectives. Research shows that diversity improves performance, including the quality of decision-making.[10]

As stated in earlier chapters, research conducted by Jim Collins revealed a common thread among the leadership of corporations whose financial performance was "great" versus "good." While it is common for fictional corporate leaders in books, movies, and on television to be portrayed as ethically challenged, bigger-than-life celebrity types, Mr. Collins's research found that a very different personality type led the most successful companies.

These highly effective corporate leaders were modest, avoided public adulation, and were never boastful, but they had strong determination and professional will. They worked very hard to accomplish tasks, and they motivated workers with standards that inspired rather than with personal charisma. Their ambition was for the company rather than for themselves, and they committed their and the organization's efforts to long-term greatness for the company. When there were failures and setbacks, the Level 5 leaders shouldered the responsibility, but when there were successes, they gave others the credit.[11] They were respectful of others.

During my years in public office, I found that the most effective political leaders who had long-term success were respectful of others, including those with whom they disagreed. Our founding fathers understood the important role mutual respect plays in the democratic process. The First Amendment to the Constitution reflects the value America places on the right to hold one's own beliefs and speak one's own mind.

I believe that one of the factors contributing to the deep political divisions in our country is a callous disrespect among individuals and groups holding differing ideologies and opinions. When we are civil in our own actions and words, we simultaneously demonstrate an appreciation for and commitment to a democratic process that depends on reasonable and reasoned discourse.

I also believe that the democratic process works better when discourse is civil rather than uncivil. S. Chris Edmonds defines civility as "a collection of positive behaviors that produce feelings of respect, dignity, and trust."[12]

Research in this area has found that civility enhances the performance of individuals, teams, and even entire organizations. In her book *Mastering Civility*, Christine Porath of Georgetown University writes, "Although civil behaviors entail treating others well, they must also reflect an underlying desire to show respect. It's not just treating someone well because you want something from them or because you're trying to serve your organization's interests. Civil behaviors are performed as a way of simply affirming norms of mutual respect and decency."[13]

Not only should the citizenry show respect for others whose opinions and beliefs are different from their own, but they should also demand respect from their public officials. Disrespectful behavior should not be tolerated, because it has a negative impact on the democratic process. Descriptions of people as "low class slobs," "pathetic," "dopey," dummy," or a "clown" make it more difficult for us to work together to find common ground in addressing our challenges.[14] Calling other nations "shithole countries" and referring to immigrants as "rapists" weaken our international standing.

True patriots do not try to silence those with whom they disagree but instead work to protect the rights of everyone. In doing so, they are showing respect for democratic values and the democratic process.

Responsibility

Combining a democratically run government and a capitalistic economic structure creates great potential for a society's long-term success because it provides individuals the freedom and opportunity to pursue their dreams and realize their potential. Government of and by the people means that individual persons are entrusted with power. The long-term success of a democratic society depends on a dedicated and principled citizenry, as well as on strong and ethical leadership. As citizens in a democracy, we have a duty to be informed, reflective, and ethical on matters of leadership selection, civic engagement, public policy, and the democratic process.

Patriotism requires the same. We clearly have our work cut out for us in this area, as reflected in an August 2018 interview conducted by Sarah McCammon of National Public Radio. While covering a political event in southern Indiana, she asked one of my fellow Hoosiers about the investigation of Russian involvement in the 2016 presidential election. The gentleman being interviewed responded, "I personally think it's a lot of white noise. I didn't vote for chief Boy Scout. I voted for someone to run my country and to be the leader of the free world and to do what I think is important. Do I care about all this other little peripheral stuff? Means absolutely nothing to me and a whole lot of people just like me."[15]

I have heard others express similar sentiment, and I believe it reflects a lack of understanding of the responsibility we have to elect leaders who will uphold the principles of democratic governance. To a patriotic American, these ethics and legal matters are not "little peripheral stuff." While the candor reflected in the interviewee's response may be refreshing, the content reflects a serious misunderstanding of the role integrity plays in democracy. United States intelligence has confirmed Russian interference in the 2016 electoral process, which means that the process was contaminated.

It is unpatriotic to ignore or to lessen the gravity of foreign intervention in our elections. Additionally, patriotism demands that we all take responsibility for holding our leaders accountable for running their campaigns and carrying out their official responsibilities with integrity.

Policy positions are not the only matters of importance to the successful running of a country. While it is not likely that we will ever see a perfect person running for office, a candidate's ethical standards matter. Upholding democratic principles, including an uncorrupted election process, is crucial to the democratic process.

At the very least, we should all read the US Constitution and understand the issues so that we can build a base of knowledge regarding our nation's democratic values and structure. The three branches of our government work independently, each with different authorities, and they serve as a check against concentration of power. They exist to protect and defend our people and our country.

For example, we each must understand the difference between questioning a judicial decision and undermining the judicial process. As expressed so well by the Brennan Center for Justice at the New York University School of Law, the president, to the detriment of our country and its democratic values,

> has displayed a troubling pattern of attacking judges and the courts for rulings he disagrees with—a pattern that began during his presidential campaign (and even before), and has continued into his presidency. This threatens our entire system of government. The courts are bulwarks of our Constitution and laws, and they depend on the public to respect their judgments and on officials to obey and enforce their decisions. Fear of personal attacks, public backlash, or enforcement failures should not color judicial decision-making, and public officials have a responsibility to respect courts and judicial decisions. Separation of powers is not a threat to democracy; it is the essence of democracy.[16]

This is an ethics issue that has long-term negative consequences for our democracy, and we must demand more from our leaders and ourselves. As we the people have the power of democracy, we must not tolerate such behavior from anyone, but especially not from those who hold the highest and most powerful positions in government. It is our patriotic duty.

We also have the responsibility to develop information literacy. All too often, people spread untruths not because they are dishonest but because they have not made the effort to validate what they have heard or read. A good example is the way some members of the public impact the political process by using social media to deliberately disseminate untruths in ways that benefit their candidates or ideology. We have the right of free speech, but it is a right that should be exercised responsibly.

When I see news stories of how social media platforms, such as Facebook or Twitter, are used to spread false information, I am reminded of a game I first played many years ago as a member of a church youth group. At one of our regular Sunday evening meetings, our youth leader introduced us to the game of telephone. We arranged our chairs in a circle, and a fellow member of our youth group was instructed to whisper a message to the person sitting adjacent to him or her. This action was repeated successively around the circle until the message reached the last person in our group. Anyone who has ever engaged in this exercise knows the process as well as the predictable result. That evening, we played several rounds of telephone, and not once did the kid at the end of the whisper chain hear something whose meaning was even close to the original message.

We were all highly amused and entertained. But the exercise also taught us a very important lesson about the ease with which one may spread falsehoods that can be harmful to others. We were reminded that truth has value. And we were taught that before we speak, we must make an honest effort to validate the accuracy of our message. This is a moral and religious value, but it is central to democratic governance. Democracy depends on honest decision-making. If we want our nation to survive and thrive, we must seek the truth and speak the truth.

If we genuinely believe that free speech plays an important role in democracy and if we recognize the importance of truth in policy-making, we will commit ourselves to fact-driven decision-making. Democracy depends on truth, but unfortunately, there are many among us who have not made that commitment. And the problem is not limited only to those who hold positions of power in our government. Far too many of our citizenry place their own interests above truth and, therefore, our country. The challenges we face are great.

In a study on the dissemination of truth and lies, it was found that lies spread more quickly and broadly than truth. Specifically, researchers at the Massachusetts Institute of Technology used a data set to track the speed and breadth of the dissemination of factual and false information through Twitter. They found that "Falsehood diffused significantly farther, faster, deeper, and more broadly than the truth in all categories of information, and the effects were more pronounced for false political news" than for false news about other topics.[17] It is not clear why people are more likely to share falsehoods than facts. It may be that fabrications tend to be more unique and interesting than truths. But there is no legitimate excuse for anyone to forward information that has not been verified, especially if it has the potential to weaken the democratic process.

Equally disconcerting is behavior that reflects an ostensible indifference to or unawareness of the fundamentals of democracy. For example, continuous denigration of news as "fake" is not merely disingenuous and self-serving. While it is quite appropriate to raise legitimate concerns about news reporting that is not accurate or balanced, assaulting a free and independent press for political gain is nothing less than an attempt to destroy a pillar of our democracy. The free dissemination of information, unabridged by the government, is the lifeblood of a democratic state; therefore, we must recognize unfounded and self-serving attacks on the media as attacks on our democracy.

True patriots value the responsibility inherent in the democratic process as much as, if not more than, their own ideology.

Fairness

A core tenet of democracy is fair distribution of power among the people. Fairness in elections is critical to this principle. We must reform our campaign finance system to include a match for small donations and to temper the power of Super PACS. And we must take the drawing of congressional maps out of the hands of the politicians and put it into the hands of nonpolitical, independent commissions.

We must also stand up to those who want to weaken organized labor; we must strike down right-to-work and other laws that undermine fairness in the workplace. Even though there is widespread agreement on the value of the fairness principle, throughout our history, the citizenry and leadership have been regularly called upon to defend it. President Lincoln's Gettysburg address exemplified leadership at its best, as he confronted the forces that threatened this principle as well as our very existence as a free and democratic nation.

At the dedication of the National Cemetery at Gettysburg, on November 19, 1863, President Lincoln very simply and eloquently reconfirmed this value of American democracy. In his two-minute address, he reminded the country of the need to hold together the union as we recognized the debt of gratitude owed to the more than 3,500 Union soldiers killed in the battle that many believe was the turning point in the Civil War.[18]

His closing words provide a poignant reminder of American values:

> It is for us, the living, rather to be dedicated here to the unfinished work which they have, thus far, so nobly carried on. It is rather for us to be here dedicated to the great task remaining before us—that from these honored dead we take increased devotion to that cause for which they here gave the last full measure of devotion—that we here highly resolve that these dead shall not have died in vain; that this nation shall have a new birth of freedom; and that this government of the people, by the people, for the people, shall not perish from the earth.[19]

It could not be clearer. Upholding the democratic value of fairness, including respect for the right of everyone to be heard and to participate and to have the opportunity to pursue their individual potential, is an act of patriotism.

To illustrate the difference between those who serve with character and those who do not, we can contrast these words of President Lincoln with the words of Congressman Steve King of Iowa. When describing the children of immigrants who have illegally entered our country, King said, "For everyone who's a valedictorian, there's another 100 out there that weigh 130 pounds and they've got calves the size of cantaloupes because they're hauling 75 pounds of marijuana across the desert."[20]

In an interview with the *New York Times*, Congressman King was quoted as asking, "White nationalist, white supremacist, Western civilization—how did that language become offensive?" Within days of the publication of that interview, the House Republican Conference stripped him of his committee assignments, and the full House adopted a resolution rejecting the words *white supremacy* and *white nationalism* as "hateful expressions of intolerance that are contradictory to the values that define the people of the United States."[21]

Racism has no place in the individual American's character, and it is unpatriotic to tolerate such bigotry from our leaders. Research not only tells us there are no correlations between genetics and intelligence; it also tells us that we are all much more genetically similar than dissimilar. Consensus in the biological and social sciences tells us that differences in skin color reflect environmental differences and that race is a social construct rather than a biological attribute.[22]

With population growth, advances in technology, increased diversity, and globalization, we are likely to find it more challenging to protect the right to fairness. The magnitude and rate of these changes clearly create changes in our environment, and that change can be uncomfortable and challenging for us.

In 1972 when I cast my first vote in a presidential election, the total population of the United States was about 209 million people, of which 87 percent were white, 11 percent were black, and less than 1 percent were Hispanic or Latino.[23] By 2018, our population had grown by more than 50 percent to a little more than 327 million people, of which 60.7 percent were white, 13.4 percent were black, and 18.1 percent were Hispanic or Latino.[24] During this same time period, we have seen a significant growth in international business relationships. According to the World Bank, the total value of world merchandise exports (priced in current US dollars) in 1960 was $122.988 billion and had grown to $17.846 trillion by 2017.[25]

It can be difficult to adjust to all the changes occurring in our communities and country. Losing our comfort zone can make us feel threatened.

Research findings indicate that increased ethnic and racial diversity can result in loss of trust in a community. More specifically, "because increasing racial diversity in majority White neighborhoods, states, and nations implies a smaller White population share, Whites may perceive these demographic changes as threatening to their status, and these changes may lead to negative racial attitudes and behavior." But over time and with sustained contact, racially diverse populations develop positive feelings and relationships toward one another.[26]

For democracy to work, we must open our minds and recognize that none of us has all the answers. And we must work together to find areas of agreement in how we solve our nation's challenges. Policy-making is a shared responsibility, and compromise has merit. While we should never negotiate away our nation's democratic principles, the democratic process requires us to make concessions. No matter how strongly I personally feel about something, it is not reasonable for me to expect my US representative or senator to always do what I want. Nor should I expect that of the entire Congress or the president.

True patriots understand that fairness of process and outcome take precedent over our individual wants.

Caring

Tolerance is more than a virtue; it is central to who we are as a people. Our founding fathers made clear that democracy provides us a space where everyone, regardless of similarities or difference, has worth. In democracy, we value individuals and their rights. The very concept of self-governance depends on a citizenry that cares about one another and is willing to fight for their rights.

Caring is central to who we are today and what we will become tomorrow. I believe that acts of compassion for others provide us the potential to be our greatest. I also believe that caring about others who come from backgrounds different than our own provides an opportunity for all of us to become stronger and better as a people. While it may be easier for us to relate to those we view as similar to ourselves, we all benefit when our compassion extends across ethnic, racial, gender, economic, geographic, and other lines.

In remarks delivered at a Presidential Medal of Freedom presentation ceremony at the end of his second term, President Ronald Reagan made clear his belief that America's strength comes from diversity. He said,

> We lead the world because, unique among nations, we draw our people—our strength—from every country and corner of the world. And by doing so we continuously renew and enrich our nation. While other countries cling to the stale past, here in America we breathe life into dreams. We create the future, and the world follows us into tomorrow. Thanks to each wave of new arrivals to this land of opportunity, we're a nation forever young, forever bursting with energy and new ideas, and always on the cutting edge, always leading the world to the next frontier. This quality is vital to our future as a nation. If we ever closed the door to new Americans, our leadership in the world would soon be lost.[27]

Not everyone agrees with me about the value of diversity. But virtually everyone agrees that diversity and globalization are a reality and that the world's population has always been diverse and on the move. According to the National Geographic's Genographic Project, human migration can be traced at least as far back as sixty thousand to seventy thousand years ago.[28] Additionally, African and European migration to the Americas dates back centuries.

There is a great deal of potential for us as a heterogeneous population. We know, for example, that workplace diversity improves performance. For example, a 2015 McKinsey report on 366 companies found that "those in the top quartile for ethnic and racial diversity in management were 35% more likely to have financial returns above the industry mean, and those in the top quartile for gender diversity were 15% more likely to have returns above the industry mean."[29]

Although I believe that diversity and globalization create opportunities, I also recognize that they create challenges. And these challenges must be taken seriously. In many ways, life is easier when our environment is familiar and simple and small. As we break down barriers between foreign populations and distant locations, our personal world becomes more complex. Thriving in a more complex environment requires us to be more educated and informed, and that requires real work.

We must hold ourselves and our leaders to a standard that recognizes democracy works only when we care about others. We the people should not tolerate the actions of an elected official describing fellow humans as "infesting our country" or as "animals." These words are not just insensitive; they are incompatible with democratic values. Anyone who would use such demeaning words demonstrates a lack of understanding of the democratic principles of equality of opportunity to participate fully in our society. In a democracy, we must care about one another, because we are all a part of something much bigger than ourselves as individuals.

True patriots understand that democracy depends on us caring about and valuing one another.

Citizenship

There should be no question that we must all hold ourselves individually responsible for good citizenship. In a 2018 survey, the Pew Research Center found that a strong majority of the American public believes the following actions are very or somewhat important to good citizenship: always following the law (96%), respecting the opinions of those who disagree (92%), paying all the taxes one owes (92%), voting in elections (91%), volunteering to help others (90%), and following what happens in government and politics (90%).[30]

Public employees are beholden to us, and if they violate the principles of democracy, it is our job to make sure they are held accountable. But as private citizens living in a democracy, we are also beholden to our country and its people. And we have a duty to hold ourselves accountable. Just as we expect public employees to uphold the law, to be responsible, and to have integrity, we must expect the same of ourselves.

The very principles of self-governance and open markets can make it difficult for us to see the corresponding responsibilities we the citizenry have that are necessary for preserving and protecting these institutions. We may come to value individualism to the exclusion of what it takes to defend the democracy that defends individualism.

I believe that many of the ills we are experiencing today, as well as many from our past, are the result of a failure to make the connection between the rights we have as individuals and the responsibility we have to be good citizens.

In an essay titled "Creating the Good Society," Claire Andre and Manuel Velasquez write of this problem. They argue that the ideal of the autonomous individual depends on a more complex understanding of the interdependence of individualism and the public good. It is a "sense of common purpose and public spirit crucial to the guidance of institutions in a democracy that is absent from our society today. A ruthless individualism, expressed primarily through a market mentality, has invaded every sphere of our lives, undermining those institutions . . . that have traditionally functioned as foci of collective purposes, history and culture. This lack of common purpose or lack of concern for the common good bodes ill for a people claiming to be a democracy."[31]

While globalization and new technologies connect us in ways that create new opportunities, they also can make us feel less personally connected to community. And they increase the complexity of our decision-making, which makes the task of democratic governance more challenging because the task of informing ourselves on relevant public policy issues requires us to gather and comprehend more information. It is increasingly difficult to write and adopt effective public policy because there are so many more variables at play; therefore, voters must make more effort to be informed on the issues.

When choosing our leaders, we must elect people who not only share our political ideology but who also understand and respect the very important role community plays in keeping our democracy strong. Of equal importance, we must continuously evaluate our own individual political ideology in the context of American character and the principles of democracy.

A democratic government is a partnership of the people. Understanding America's character helps us to understand the attributes that are important to the individual American's character. For democracy to flourish, the citizenry must understand the values encompassed by this form of self-governance. And we must all be committed to upholding those shared values. Even though we regularly disagree with one another on many issues, we implicitly agree to accept and share these broader values.

In their book *How Democracies Die*, Harvard professors Steven Levitsky and Daniel Ziblatt write that we cannot merely depend on the good character of our leaders; we need norms or shared codes of conduct that are "accepted, respected, and enforced."[32] Norms can be informal, but they can also be formalized into formal codes of ethics or public laws. We can each have an individual code of behavior, but we are also bound by the values of American democracy. More than any other form of government, democracy demands a high-level commitment to good behavior and accountability from the citizenry. Without good citizenship, we cannot be our best democracy.

True patriots hold not just their leaders but also themselves to the highest standards of citizenship.

Like physical pillars that are crucial to the support of a material structure, the pillars of character are crucial to democracy. Fairness of process, trustworthiness of the people and leadership, respect and caring for others who share our world, taking responsibility for ourselves and our country, and making our best effort to be good citizens—these are the very things that keep our democracy from crumbling. I believe that at this critical time in our nation's history, we must all rededicate ourselves to these underlying values that make democracy work and make America great.

CONCLUSION

Strength of Character, Strength of Union

*We all need to do our part, to push and pull together, to make a difference in
our society. Democracy is not a state; it is an act. We must all stay in the continuing struggle to create a Beloved Community, a nation and a world society
at peace with itself.*

THE HONORABLE JOHN LEWIS[1]

WITH THESE WORDS, CONGRESSMAN JOHN Lewis appeals to our better
selves. "Pushing and pulling together" are responsibilities we have as partici-
pants in a democratic process. In democracy, we hold equal rights, and we are
each accountable for protecting these rights. When we work together and share
responsibilities and resources, we can address challenges in ways that work for
the greater good of the people, and we expand opportunities for all. The process
itself gives us strength, and we must never forget the role ethics play in protecting and preserving this process.

My country has provided me opportunities beyond anything I could have
ever imagined. I was honored to serve in Congress and the executive branch
with many men and women whose personal integrity and tireless efforts made
us stronger and better. I continue to have the privilege of working in higher education with people whose research and teaching are advancing knowledge that
leads us to better decision-making as we address today's and tomorrow's challenges. Over the years, I have learned a great deal from my respected colleagues.

But colleagues are not the only ones who have broadened my perspective
and understanding of the world. Most of what I have learned has come from

family, neighbors, constituents, and students, as well as my own teachers and professors. There is so much to learn from others who are in a different stage or walk of life. To be our strongest, we must never overlook or squander what others have to offer. Only when everyone has a place at the table can we be our best as a people.

Working together with honesty and commitment makes us strong. Over and over again, research shows that group decision-making gives us better results than individual decision-making. Groups comprised of people with diverse backgrounds and experiences make better decisions than groups with similar backgrounds and experiences. We have a great deal to learn from one another, and the democratic process recognizes the value of diversity in policy-making and implementation. Congressman John Lewis is right. We must push and pull together to make a difference in our society. We must move forward as one people.

As Aristotle taught, when we make a habit of behaving virtuously, we become people of virtue, and that leads us to successful and fulfilling lives. I am convinced that the same is true for a nation. The more character we demonstrate in running our democracy, the more character we will have as a nation and the stronger we will be. Moving forward, we will continue to encounter challenges that put this great nation's foundation and endurance at risk. We must be relentless in our efforts to minimize conflicts of interest among public servants and to advance fairness and inclusivity for our people. To be our strongest, we must hold ourselves and our leaders to the highest ethical standards that protect the process and essence of democracy.

We must work together to elect people whose policies we believe are good for our country and who also understand the importance of ethics for ensuring a fair and democratic process. And we must move forward with integrity and dedication, as a community, to protect and save America's character. That is the only way we will protect and save this great experiment in democracy, the place and people who are the United States of America.

NOTES

INTRODUCTION

1. "Roosevelt the Writer," Theodore Roosevelt Rotunda, American Museum of Natural History, accessed May 9, 2019, https://www.amnh.org/exhibitions/permanent/roosevelt-rotunda.

2. Irving L. Janis, Donald Kaye, and Paul Kirschner, "Facilitating Effects of 'Eating-While Reading' on Responsiveness to Persuasive Communications," *Journal of Personality and Social Psychology* 1, no. 2 (February 1965): 181–6.

3. Glenn Kessler, "A Year of Unprecedented Deception: Trump Averaged 15 False Claims a Day in 2018," *Washington Post*, December 30, 2018.

4. Lee Edwards, "The Massive Lies of Past Presidents Make Trump Look Honest," Heritage Foundation, August 24, 2018, https://www.heritage.org/conservatism/commentary/the-massive-lies-past-presidents-make-trump-look-honest; originally appeared in the *Federalist*.

5. Glenn Kessler, "Democrats Seize on Cherry-picked Claim That 'Medicare-for-All' Would Save $2 Trillion," *Washington Post*, August 7, 2018.

6. Aaron Blake, "Alexandria Ocasio-Cortez's Very Bad Defense of Her Falsehoods," *Washington Post*, January 7, 2019.

7. Blake, "Alexandria Ocasio-Cortez's Very Bad Defense."

8. Max H. Bazerman and Ann E. Tenbrunsel, "Stumbling into Bad Behavior," *New York Times*, April 20, 2011.

9. "Confidence in Institutions," Gallup, accessed May 10, 2019, http://news.gallup.com/poll/1597/confidence-institutions.aspx?version=print.

10. Paolo Mauro, "Corruption and Growth," *Quarterly Journal of Economics* 110, no. 3 (August 1995): 681–712.

11. Marie Chene, "The Impact of Corruption on Growth and Inequality," Transparency International, March 15, 2014, https://www.transparency.org /whatwedo/answer/the_impact_of_corruption_on_growth_and_inequality.

12. Cheol Liu and John L. Mikesell, "The Impact of Public Officials' Corruption on the Size and Allocation of U.S. State Spending," *Public Administration Review* 74, no. 3 (May/June 2014): 346–59.

13. Cheol Liu, Tima T. Moldogaziev, and John L. Mikesell, "Corruption and State and Local Government Debt Expansion," *Public Administration Review* 77, no. 5 (September/October 2017): 681–90.

14. "The S.W.A.M.P. Index 2018," Coalition for Integrity, accessed May 10, 2019, https://swamp.coalitionforintegrity.org.

15. Barb Berggoetz, "Indiana Gets D- Grade in 2015 State Integrity Investigation," Center for Public Integrity, November 9, 2015, updated November 12, 2015, https://www.publicintegrity.org/accountability/indiana-gets-d-grade-in-2015 -state-integrity-investigation/.

16. "State Trends in Child Well-Being, 2018 Kids Count Data Book," Annie E. Casey Foundation, accessed May 10, 2019, https://www.aecf.org/resources/2018 -kids-count-data-book/.

17. D. Michael Long, Christi Wann, and Christopher Brockman, "Unethical Business Behavior and Stock Performance," *Academy of Accounting and Financial Studies Journal* 20, no. 3 (2016): 115–22.

CHAPTER 1: AMERICAN CHARACTER

1. Dwight D. Eisenhower Presidential Library, Museum and Boyhood Home, National Archives, accessed May 10, 2019, http://www.eisenhower.archives.gov /all_about_ike/quotes.html.

2. Tom Brokaw, *The Greatest Generation* (New York: Random House, 2005), xxvii.

3. "America's Wars," US Department of Veterans Affairs, accessed May 10, 2019, https:/www.va.gov/opa/publications/factsheets/fs_americas_wars.pdf.

4. "Moral Character," *Stanford Encyclopedia of Philosophy*, January 15, 2003, revised April 15, 2019, https://plato.stanford.edu/entries/moral-character/.

5. "Moral Character."

6. Paul M. Johnson, "A Glossary of Political Economy Terms: Democracy," Paul M. Johnson, accessed May 14, 2019, http://webhome.auburn.edu/~johnspm /gloss/democracy.

7. Josiah Ober, "The Original Meaning of 'Democracy': Capacity to Do Things, Not Majority Rule," *Ancient History Encyclopedia*, November 7, 2011, https://www .ancient.eu/article/266/.

8. "Democracy," *Stanford Encyclopedia of Philosophy*, July 27, 2006, https://plato .stanford.edu/entries/democracy.

9. Paul M. Johnson, "A Glossary of Political Economy Terms: Communism," accessed May 14, 2019, http://webhome.auburn.edu/~johnspm/gloss/communism.

10. Angus Maddison, "The West and the Rest in the International Economic Order," OECD Observer, accessed May 14, 2019, http://oecdobserver.org/news/archivestory.php/aid/884/The_West_and_the_Rest_in_the_International_Economic_Order.html. This article is an adapted extract from Angus Maddison's chapter "The West and the Rest in the International Economic Order," in *Development Is Back* (Paris: OECD Development Centre, 2002), 31–46.

11. "Capitalism," Columbia Center on Capitalism and Society, accessed May 28, 2019, https://capitalism.columbia.edu/glossary-0.

12. Sarwat Jahan and Ahmed Saber Mahmud, "What Is Capitalism?: Free Markets May Not Be Perfect but They Are Probably the Best Way to Organize an Economy," *Finance and Development* 52, no. 2 (June 2015): 44–5.

13. Era Dabla-Norris et al., "Causes and Consequences of Income Inequality: A Global Perspective," International Monetary Fund Staff Discussion Notes, June 15, 2015, https://www.imf.org/external/pubs/ft/sdn/2015/sdn1513.pdf.

14. "The Six Pillars of Character," Josephson Institute, accessed May 14, 2019, https://www.josephsoninstitute.org/med-introtoc/.

15. Hannah Levitt and Peter Blumberg, "Wells Fargo Hits More Bumps as It Tries to Move Past Scandals," Bloomberg, March 20, 2019, https://www.bloomberg.com/news/articles/2019-03-20/wells-fargo-hits-more-bumps-as-it-tries-to-move-past-scandals.

16. "Americans with Disabilities Act Passes Senate Overwhelmingly," *Leadership Conference Education Fund Civil Rights Monitor* 4, no. 3 (Fall 1989), accessed January 8, 2019, http://www.civilrights.org/edfund/civil-rights-monitor/.

17. "About Tammy," Tammy Duckworth US Senator for Illinois, accessed May 14, 2019, https://duckworth.senate.gov/about-tammy/biography.

18. Peter Slevin, "After War Injury, an Iraq Vet Takes on Politics," *Washington Post*, February 19, 2006.

19. "And the Band Played On . . . While the Ship Sank Around Them," *US Department of Defense Standards of Conduct Office Encyclopedia of Ethical Failure*, 48–9, revised September 2018, ogc.osd.mil/defense_ethics/resource_library/eef_2019.pdf.

20. "Careers," Starbucks, accessed May 15, 2019, https://starbucks.com/careers/working-at-starbucks/benefits-and-perks.

21. "Child Protection from Violence, Exploitation and Abuse," UNICEF, accessed May 15, 2019, https://www.unicef.org/protection/57929_child_labour.html.

22. "Who We Are: Our History," Kellogg Company, accessed May 15, 2019, https://www.kelloggs.com/en_US/who-we-are/our-history.html.

23. "Who We Are: Overview," W. K. Kellogg Foundation, accessed May 15, 2019, https://wkkf.org/who-we-are/overview?#history-and-legacy.

24. "King Encyclopedia: Sit-Ins," Martin Luther King Jr. Research and Education Institute, accessed May 15, 2019, https://kinginstitute.stanford.edu/encyclopedia/sit-ins.

25. "The Definition of Morality," *Stanford Encyclopedia of Philosophy*, April 17, 2002, revised February 8, 2016, https://plato.stanford.edu/entries/morality-definition/.

26. Manuel Valasquez et al., "What Is Ethics?" Markkula Center for Applied Ethics, August 18, 2015, https://www.scu.edu/ethics/ethics-resources/ethical-decision-making/what-is-ethics/. This piece originally appeared in *Issues in Ethics* 1, no. 1 (Fall 1987) and was revised in 2010.

27. "Code of Ethics," Society of Professional Journalists, accessed May 15, 2019, https://www.spj.org/pdf/spj-code-of-ethics.pdf.

28. "Code of Ethics."

29. "Inaugural Address of the President, March 4, 1933," National Archives, accessed May 15, 2019, https://www.archives.gov/education/lessons/fdr-inaugural.

30. Steven E. Haugen, "Measures of Labor Underutilization from the Current Population Survey," Bureau of Labor Statistics, US Department of Labor, March 2009, https://www.bls.gov/osmr/research-papers/2009/pdf/ec090020.pdf.

31. "Eighty Years after the Reciprocal Trade Agreement Act," Tradewinds, Office of the US Trade Representative, June 2014, https://ustr.gov/about-us/policy-offices/press-office/blog/2014/June/Eighty-years-of-the-Reciprocal-Trade-Agreements-Act.

32. "Executive Order 8802: Prohibition of Discrimination in the Defense Industry (1941)," US National Archives and Records Administration, accessed May 15, 2019, http://www.ourdocuments.gov/doc.php?doc=72.

33. "History of the Marshall Plan," George C. Marshall Foundation, accessed May 15, 2019, http://www.marshallfoundation.org/marshall/the-marshall-plan/history-marshall-plan/.

34. "Combating Corruption," World Bank, updated October 4, 2018, www.worldbank.org/en/topic/governance/brief/anti-corruption.

35. Cheol Liu and John L. Mikesell, "The Impact of Public Officials' Corruption on the Size and Allocation of U.S. State Spending," *Public Administration Review* 74, no. 3 (May/June 2014): 346–59.

36. Surendranath R. Jory et al., "The Market Response to Corporate Scandals Involving CEOs," *Applied Economics* 47, no. 17 (2015): 1723–38.

37. Michelle Park Lazette, "Nonprofits Hit by Bad Publicity Are More 'Fragile' Than For-Profit Counterparts," *Crain's Cleveland Business*, October 27, 2013, https://www.crainscleveland.com/article/20131027/SUB1/310279979/nonprofits-hit-by-bad-publicity-are-more-fragile-than-for-profit.

38. Steven Balsam and Erica E. Harris, "The Impact of CEO Compensation on Nonprofit Donations," *Accounting Review* 89, no. 2 (March 2014): 425–50, https://aaapubs.org/doi/10.2308/accr-50631.

39. Rich Morin, "The Price That Politicians Pay for Scandals," Fact Tank, Pew Research Center, July 18, 2013, https://www.pewresearch.org/fact-tank/2013/07/18/the-price-that-politicians-pay-for-scandals. This is a summary of research conducted by Praino, Stockemer, and Moscardelli.

40. "Public Trust in Government: 1958–2019," Pew Research Center, April 11, 2019, https://www.people-press.org/2019/04/11/public-trust-in-government-1958-2019/.

41. Laura Kurtzman, "With a Free Meal from Pharma, Doctors Are More Likely to Prescribe Brand-Name Drugs, Study Shows," University of California San Francisco, June 20, 2016, https://www.ucsf.edu/news/2016/06/403306/free-meal-pharma-doctors-are-more-likely-prescribe-brand-name-drugs-study-shows. This is a summary of research conducted by DeJong and Aguilar.

42. "Code of Medical Ethics Opinion 9.6.2," American Medical Association, accessed May 16, 2019, https://www.ama-assn.org/delivering-care/ethics/gifts-physicians-industry.

CHAPTER 2: DECISION-MAKING WITH CHARACTER

1. "Abraham Lincoln Quotes," Abraham Lincoln Center for Character Development, accessed May 16, 2019, https://alccd.lincolncollege.edu/resources/.

2. "Slaying the Dragon of Debt: Fiscal Politics and Policy from the 1970s to the Present," Regional Oral History Office, Bancroft Library, University of California Berkeley, accessed May 16, 2019, bancroft.berkeley.edu/ROHO/projects/debt/budgetenforcementact.html.

3. Nick Rasmussen, "The Weight of One Mission: Recounting the Death of Usama bin Laden, Five Years Later," White House, accessed May 16, 2019, https://obamawhitehouse.archives.gov/blog/2016/05/02/weight-one-mission-recounting-death-usama-bin-laden-five-years-later.

4. Jim Collins, "Level 5 Leadership," Jim Collins, accessed May 17, 2019, https://www.jimcollins.com/concepts/level-five-leadership.html.

5. Collins, "Level 5 Leadership."

6. Lawrence Kohlberg, "The Child as a Moral Philosopher," *Psychology Today* 2, no. 4 (September 1968): 24–30.

7. Kohlberg, "Child as a Moral Philosopher."

8. "Rod Blagojevich Public Corruption Case," *Inside the FBI*, March 12, 2012, https://www.fbi.gov/audio-repository/news-podcasts-inside-rod-blagojevich-public-corruption-case.mp3/view.

9. "Behavioral Ethics," Ethics Unwrapped, McCombs School of Business, University of Texas, accessed May 17, 2019, https://ethicsunwrapped.utexas.edu /subject-area/behavioral-ethics.

10. Julia A. Files et al., "Speaker Introductions at Internal Medicine Grand Rounds: Forms of Address Reveal Gender Bias," *Journal of Women's Health* 26, no. 5 (2017): 413–9.

11. Tonja Jacobi and Dylan Schweers, "Justice, Interrupted: The Effect of Gender, Ideology, and Seniority at Supreme Court Oral Arguments," *Virginia Law Review* 103, no. 7 (November 2017): 1379–96.

12. "Politics Is Personal: Keys to Likeability and Electability for Women," Barbara Lee Family Foundation, April 2016, https://www.barbaraleefoundation.org /wp-content/uploads/BLFF-Likeability-Memo-FINAL.pdf.

13. John R. Graham, Campbell R. Harvey, and Manju Puri, "A Corporate Beauty Contest," Fuqua School of Business, Duke University and National Bureau of Economic Research, March 2010, https://faculty.fuqua.duke.edu/~charvey /Research/Working_Papers/W101_A_corporate_beauty.pdf.

14. Claire Zillman, "The Fortune 500 Has More Female CEOs Than Ever Before," *Fortune*, May 16, 2019, fortune.com/2019/05/16/fortune-500-female-ceos/.

CHAPTER 3: THE HABIT OF LEADING WITH CHARACTER

1. "Remembering Dr. Martin Luther King, Jr.," Maria Cantwell US Senator for Washington, January 17, 2005, https://www.cantwell.senate.gov/news/press -releases/remembering-dr-martin-luther-king-jr.

2. Julie Ray, "World's Approval of U.S. Leadership Drops to New Low," Gallup, January 18, 2018, https://news.gallup.com/poll/225761/world-approval-leadership -drops-new-low.aspx.

3. Richard Wike et al., "Trump's International Ratings Remain Low, Especially Among Key Allies," Pew Research Center, October 1, 2018, https://www .pewglobal.org/2018/10/01/trumps-international-ratings-remain-low-especially -among-key-allies/.

4. Oliver J. Sheldon and Ayelet Fishbach, "Anticipating and Resisting the Temptation to Behave Unethically," *Personality and Social Psychology Bulletin*, received October 31, 2014, revised April 19, 2015, Sage Publications, journals.sagepub .com/doi/10.1177/0146167215586196.

5. "About the U.S. Department of State," US Department of State, accessed May 17, 2019, https://www.state.gov/about/about-the-u-s-department-of-state.

6. "Our Story," US Department of Defense, accessed May 17, 2019, https:// www.defense.gov/Our-Story/.

7. "About HHS," US Department of Health and Human Services, accessed May 17, 2019, https://www.hhs.gov/about/index.html.

8. "Staying Focused, Going Further," Kellogg Company, accessed May 17, 2019, https://www.kelloggcompany.com/en_US/our-vision-purpose.html.

9. "About Microsoft," Microsoft, accessed May 17, 2019, https://www.microsoft.com/en-us/about.

10. "Our Purpose," Eli Lilly and Company, accessed May 17, 2019, https://www.lilly.com/who-we-are.

11. Drew Hendricks, "Personal Mission Statement of 13 CEOs and Lessons You Need to Learn," *Forbes*, November 10, 2014, https://forbes.com/sites/drewhendricks/2014/11/10/personal-mission-statement-of-14-ceos-and-lessons-you-need-to-learn/#373d797b1e5e.

12. Hendricks, "Personal Mission Statement."

13. Timothy L. Fort, *The Vision of the Firm: Its Governance, Obligations, and Aspirations* (St. Paul, MN: West Academic Publishing, 2014), 68–76.

14. Jeffrey M. Jones, "Job Approval of Congress Reaches Two-Year High," Gallup, March 19, 2019, https://news.gallup.com/poll/247928/job-approval-congress-reaches-two-year-high.aspx.

15. Kenneth S. Pope, "Steps to Strengthen Ethics in Organizations: Research Findings, Ethics Placebos, and What Works," *Journal of Trauma & Dissociation* 16, no. 2 (March 15, 2015): 139–52.

CHAPTER 4: ETHICS AND DEMOCRACY

1. "Inaugural Address of President John F. Kennedy," John F. Kennedy Presidential Library and Museum, accessed May 18, 2019, https://www.jfklibrary.org/learn/about-jfk/historic-speeches/inaugural-address.

2. Associated Press, "Convictions in the Abramoff Corruption Probe," CBS News, February 11, 2011, https://www.cbsnews.com/news/convictions-in-the-abramoff-corruption-probe/.

3. Jack Maskell, "Financial Disclosure by Federal Officials and Publication of Disclosure Reports," Congressional Research Service, August 22, 2013.

4. Jack Maskell, "The STOCK Act, Insider Trading, and Public Financial Reporting by Federal Officials," Congressional Research Service, April 18, 2013.

5. "Presidential Tax Returns," Tax History Project, accessed May 18, 2019, taxhistory.tax.org.

6. "Definitions," Issues of Democracy, University of Notre Dame, https://www3.nd.edu/~amcadams/CAPP485/StudentWebPages/democracy/democracy/definition.html.

7. "Gettysburg Address," National Archives, accessed May 18, 2019, https://www.ourdocuments.gov/doc.php?flash=false&doc=36&page=transcript.

8. Lynn S. Paine, "Managing for Organizational Integrity," *Harvard Business Review*, March–April, 1994, https://hbr.org/1994/03/managing-for-organizational-integrity.

9. "Executive Orders Disposition Tables," National Archives, accessed May 18, 2019, https://www.archives.gov/federal-register/executive-orders/1989-bush.html.

10. "The 14 General Principles of Ethical Conduct," Office of Government Ethics, accessed May 18, 2019, https://www.oge.gov/Web/OGE.nsf/0/73636C89FB09 28DB8525804B005605A5/$FILE/14%20General%20Priniciples.pdf.

11. Richard Painter, "Ethics and Government Lawyering in Current Times," speech delivered at Hofstra Law as a Howard Lichtenstein Annual Lecture, February 26, 2018, accessed May 18, 2019, https://www.hofstralawreview.org/wp -content/uploads/2019/05/cc.1.painter.pdf.

12. Jack Maskell, "The Receipt of Gifts by Federal Employees in the Executive Branch," Congressional Research Service, December 5, 2014.

13. Jennifer Wang, "Why Trump Won't Use a Blind Trust and What His Predecessors Did with Their Assets," *Forbes,* November 15, 2016, https://www.forbes .com/sites/jenniferwang/2016/11/15/why-trump-wont-use-a-blind-trust-and-what -his-predecessors-did-with-their-assets/#38fce6129c0.

14. MCE, "Conflicts of Interest and the President: Reviewing the State of Law in the Face of a Trump Presidency," *Emory Corporate Governance and Accountability Review* 4 (2017): 47–59, law.emory.edu/ecgar/content/volume-4/issue-special /essays-interviews/conflicts-president-law-trump-presidency.html.

15. "Former Postmaster General Pays Settlement to End Conflict Investigation," *Encyclopedia of Ethical Failure,* 51–2, revised September 2018, ogc.osd.mil/defense _ethics/resource_library/eef_2019.pdf.

16. "Awarding Contracts to Spouse, II," *Encyclopedia of Ethical Failure,* 48, revised September 2018, ogc.osd.mil/defense_ethics/resource_library/eef.2019.pdf.

17. "Congressional Ethics Reform Act—H.R. 2735, 103rd Congress (1993– 1994)," Congress.gov, accessed May 20, 2019, https://www.congress.gov/bill/103rd /house-bill/2735.

18. "Jill Lynette Long," History, Art, and Archives, US House of Representatives, accessed May 20, 2019, https://history.house.gov/People/Detail/17117.

19. "Highlights of the House Ethics Rules," Committee on Ethics, US House of Representatives, accessed May 20, 2019, https://ethics.house.gov//publications /highlights-house-ethics-rules; and "An Overview of the Senate Code of Conduct and Related Laws," Select Committee on Ethics, US Senate, accessed November 21, 2019, https://www.ethics.senate.gov/public/index.cfm/files/serve?File_id =1aec2c45-aadf-46e3-bb36-c472bcbed20f.

20. "Highlights of the House Ethics Rules"; and "Overview of the Senate Code."

21. Hunter Schwarz, "More Than Two Dozen Members of Congress Have Been Indicted Since 1980," *Washington Post,* July 29, 2015, https://www.washingtonpost .com/news/the-fix/wp/2015/07/29/more-than-two-dozen-members-of-congress -have-been-indicted-since-1980/?utm_term=.9c1ef1f302a0.

22. "Code of Conduct for United States Judges," US Courts, accessed May 20, 2019, https://www.uscourts.gov/judges-judgeships/code-conduct-united-states-judges.

23. "About the Commission," US Sentencing Commission, accessed May 20, 2019, https://www.ussc.gov.

24. Sonja B. Starr, "Estimating Gender Disparities in Federal Criminal Cases," *Law & Economics Working Papers*, paper 57 (September 14, 2012), https://repository.law.umich.edu/cgi/viewcontent.cgi?article=1164&context=law_econ_current.

25. Sonja B. Starr and Marit M. Rehavi, "Racial Disparity in Federal Criminal Sentences," *Journal of Political Economy* 122, no. 6 (December 2014): 1320–54, https://repository.law.umich.edu/cgi/viewcontent.cgi?article=2413&context=articles.

26. Michele L. Jawando and Allie Anderson, "Racial and Gender Diversity Sorely Lacking in America's Courts," Center for American Progress, September 15, 2016, https://www.americanprogress.org/issues/courts/news/2016/09/15/144287/racial-and-gender-diversity-sorely-lacking-in-americas-courts/.

27. Maria Kimberly, "House of Burgesses," Mount Vernon, accessed May 20, 2019, https://www.mountvernon.org/library/digitalhistory/digital-encyclopedia/article/house-of-burgesses/.

28. Richard C. Stazesky, "George Washington, Genius in Leadership," Washington Papers, University of Virginia, accessed May 20, 2019, gwpapers.virginia.edu/resources/articles/george-washington-genius-in-leadership/.

29. Jay Richardson, "Cherry Tree Myth," Mount Vernon, accessed May 20, 2019, https://www.mountvernon.org/library/digitalhistory/digital-encyclopedia/article/cherry-tree-myth/.

30. "Guides," Federal Election Commission, accessed May 20, 2019, https://www.fec.gov/help-candidates-and-committees/guides/.

31. Maury Klein, "First PAC Used $600,000 to Elect Roosevelt, Boost Unions," Bloomberg, October 10, 2012, https://www.bloomberg.com/view/articles/2012-10-10/first-pac-used-600-000-to-elect-roosevelt-boost-unions.

32. "Money in Politics Timeline," Open Secrets, accessed May 20, 2019, https://www.opensecrets.org/resources/learn/timeline.

33. "Contributions to Super PACs and Hybrid PACs," Federal Election Commission, accessed May 20, 2019, https://www.fec.gov/help-candidates-and-committees/taking-receipts-pac/contributions-to-super-pacs-and-hybrid-pacs/.

34. Molly E. Reynolds, "Republicans in Congress Got a 'Seats Bonus' This Election (Again)," Brookings Institution, November 22, 2016, https://www.brookings.edu/blog/fixgov/2016/11/22/gop-seats-bonus-in-congress/.

35. Reynolds, "Republicans in Congress."

36. Laura Royden, Michael Li, and Yuri Rudensky, "Extreme Gerrymandering and the 2018 Midterm," Brennan Center for Justice, New York University School of Law, March 23, 2018, https://www.brennancenter.org/publication/extreme -gerrymandering-2018-midterm.

37. "New Voting Restrictions in America," Brennan Center for Justice, New York University School of Law, accessed May 21, 2019, https://www.brennancenter .org/new-voting-restrictions-america.

38. Lorraine C. Minnite, "The Politics of Voter Fraud," Project Vote, accessed May 21, 2019, www.projectvote.org/wp-content/uploads/2007/03/Politics_of _Voter_Fraud_Final.pdf.

39. Minnite, "Politics of Voter Fraud."

40. John F. Kennedy, "Radio and Television Report to the American People on Civil Rights, June 11, 1963," John F. Kennedy Presidential Library and Museum, ac- cessed May 21, 2019, https://www.jfklibrary.org/archives/other-resources/john -f-kennedy-speeches/civil-rights-radio-and-television-report-19630611.

CHAPTER 5: DEMOCRACY, ETHICS, AND CAPITALISM

1. Franklin D. Roosevelt, "The New Deal—Message to Congress on the Con- centration of Economic Power," April 29, 1938, Pepperdine School of Public Policy, accessed May 21, 2019, https://publicpolicy.pepperdine.edu/academics/research /faculty-research/new-deal/roosevelt-speeches/fr042938.htm.

2. Milton Friedman, "The Social Responsibility of Business Is to Increase Its Profits," *New York Times Magazine*, September 13, 1970, umich.edu~thecore/doc /Friedman.pdf.

3. Ioanna Boulouta and Christos N. Pitelis, "Who Needs CSR?: The Impact of Corporate Social Responsibility on National Competitiveness," *Journal of Business Ethics* 119, no. 3 (February 3, 2013): 349–64.

4. Andrew Kassoy, Bart Houlahan, and Jay Coen Gilbert, "Impact Governance and Management: Fulfilling the Promise of Capitalism to Achieve a Shared and Durable Prosperity," Brookings Institution, July 1, 2016, https://www.brookings .edu/research/impact-governance-and-management-fulfilling-the-promise-of -capitalism-to-achieve-a-shared-and-durable-prosperity/.

5. Friedman, "Social Responsibility of Business."

6. Ruben Hernandez-Murillo and Christopher J. Martinek, "Corporate Social Responsibility Can Be Profitable," Federal Reserve Bank of St. Louis, April 1, 2009, https://www.stlouisfed.org/publications/regional-economist/april-2009 /corporate-social-responsibility-can-be-profitable.

7. Angus Maddison, "The West and the Rest in the International Economic Order," OECD Observer, accessed May 21, 2019, oecdobserver.org/news/

archivestory.php/aid/884/The_West_and_the_Rest_in_the_International
_Economic_Order.html. This article is an adapted extract from Angus Maddison's
chapter "The West and the Rest in the International Economic Order," in *Development Is Back* (Paris: OECD Development Centre, 2002), 31–46.

8. "Gini Index for the United States," Federal Reserve Bank of St. Louis, updated April 25, 2018, https://fred.stlouisfed.org/series/SIPOVGINIUSA.

9. "Gini Index for the United States."

10. Eric D. Gould and Alexander Hijzen, "In Equality, We Trust," *Finance and Development* 54, no. 1 (March 2017): 37–9, https://www.imf.org/external/pubs/ft/fandd/2017/03/pdf/gould.pdf.

11. Gould and Hijzen, "In Equality, We Trust."

12. Henry Farber et al., "Unions and Inequality over the Twentieth Century: New Evidence from Survey Data," OpenScholar @ Princeton, December 4, 2017, https://scholar.princeton.edu/sites/default/files/kuziemko/files/union_ineq_4dec2017.pdf.

13. Lawrence Mishel and Jessica Schieder, "CEO Compensation Surged in 2017," Economic Policy Institute, August 16, 2018, https://www.epi.org/publication/ceo-compensation-surged-in-2017/.

14. John DiNardo and David S. Lee, "Do Unions Cause Business Failures?," March 2003, https://www.princeton.edu/~davidlee/wp/unionbf.pdf.

15. Jason Perry and Patrick de Fontnouvelle, "Measuring Reputational Risk: The Market Reaction to Operational Loss Announcements," Federal Reserve Bank of Boston, October 2005, https://www.bostonfed.org/people/bank/patrick-de-fontnouvelle.aspx.

16. Barry Eichengreen, "Financial Crisis: Revisiting the Banking Rules That Died by a Thousand Small Cuts," *Fortune,* January 16, 2015, fortune.com/2015/01/16/financial-crisis-bank-regulation.

17. Jihad Dagher, "Regulatory Cycles: Revisiting the Political Economy of Financial Crises," International Monetary Fund, January 15, 2018, https://www.imf.org/en/Publications/WP/Issues/2018/01/15/Regulatory-Cycles-Revisiting-the-Political-Economy-of-Financial-Crises-45562.

18. Erika Andersen, "23 Quotes from Warren Buffett on Life and Generosity," *Forbes,* December 2, 2013, https://www.forbes.com/sites/erikaandersen/2013/12/02/23-quotes-from-warren-buffett-on-life-and-generosity/#562aebf891.

19. "Corporate Codes of Conduct," Federal Deposit Insurance Corporation, accessed May 21, 2019, https://www.fdic.gov/news/news/financial/2005/fil10505a.html.

20. "Understanding Deposit Insurance," Federal Deposit Insurance Corporation, accessed May 21, 2019, https://www.fdic.gov/deposit/deposits.

21. "Understanding Deposit Insurance."

22. "Darwin E. Smith," International Hall of Fame, Discovery Center, accessed December 1, 2019, https://www.paperdiscoverycenter.org/halloffame/2018/12/28 /darwin-smith.

23. Friedman, "Social Responsibility of Business."

CHAPTER 6: THE AMERICAN'S CHARACTER

1. "The Consumer Era, 1940s–1970s," National Museum of American History, Smithsonian, accessed May 21, 2019, https://americanhistory.si.edu/american -enterprise-exhibition/consumer-era.

2. "Jim Crow Laws and Racial Segregation," Social Welfare History Project, Virginia Commonwealth University, accessed May 21, 2019, https://socialwelfare .library.vcu.edu/eras/civil-war-reconstructiobn/jim-crow-laws-andracial -segregation/.

3. Jordan Moran, "Nixon and the Pentagon Papers," Miller Center, University of Virginia, accessed May 22, 2019, https://millercenter.org/the-presidency /educational-resources/first-domino-nixon-and-the-pentagon-papers.

4. Ford Foundation, "Veterans, Deserters, and Draft-Evaders—The Vietnam Decade," Charles E. Goodell Papers, Gerald R. Ford Presidential Library, accessed May 22, 2019, https://www.fordlibrarymuseum.gov/library/document/0193 /1505994.pdf.

5. "President Lincoln," National Endowment for the Humanities, accessed May 22, 2019, https://edsitement.neh.gov/this-day/president-lincoln-shot.

6. Jennifer Epstein, "Trump Faces Laughter at UN, Then Unleashes Global Grievances List," Bloomberg, September 25, 2018, https://www.bloomberg.com /news/articles/2018-09-25/trump-faces-laughter-at-un-then-unleashes-global -grievance-list.

7. "A Fiscal Year Defined by $2.4 Trillion in New Debt," Committee for a Responsible Federal Budget, September 28, 2018, https://www.crfb.org/blogs/fiscal -year-defined-24-trillion-new-debt.

8. Lorraine C. Minnite, "The Politics of Voter Fraud," Project Vote, accessed May 22, 2019, www.projectvote.org/wp-content/uploads/2007/03/Politics_of _Voter_Fraud_Final.pdf.

9. Jocelyn Benson and Michael T. Morley, "The Twenty-Sixth Amendment," National Constitution Center, accessed May 22, 2019, https://constitutioncenter .org/interactive-constitution/amendments/amendment-xxvi.

10. David Rock and Heidi Grant, "Why Diverse Teams Are Smarter," *Harvard Business Review*, November 4, 2016, https://hbr.org/2016/11/why-diverse-teams -are-smarter.

11. Jim Collins, "Level 5 Leadership," Jim Collins, accessed May 22, 2019, https://www.jimcollins.com/concepts/level-five-leadership.html.

12. S. Chris Edmonds, "Four Steps Proven to Cultivate Workplace Civility," *Forbes*, April 14, 2017, https://www.forbes.com/sites/forbescoachescouncil/2017/04/14/four-steps-proven-to-cultivate-workplace-civility/#d01f89c37cf4.

13. Christine Porath, *Mastering Civility* (New York: Grand Central, 2016), 27.

14. "Donald Trump's 10 Most Offensive Tweets," *Forbes*, accessed November 21, 2019, https://www.forbes.com/pictures/flji45elmm/donald-trumps-10-most-of/#5f83f7b370df.

15. Sarah McCammon, "In Indiana, Trump's Supporters Remain Loyal Despite Legal Troubles," *All Things Considered*, August 31, 2018, https://www.npr.org/2018/08/31/643798726/in-indiana-trumps-supporters-remain-loyal-desppite-legal-troubles.

16. "In His Own Words: The President's Attacks on the Courts," Brennan Center for Justice, New York University School of Law, June 5, 2017, https://www.brennancenter.org/analysis/his-own-words-presidents-attacks-courts.

17. Soroush Vosoughi, Deb Roy, and Sinan Aral, "The Spread of True and False News Online," *Science* 359, no. 6380 (March 9, 2018): 1146–51, https://science.sciencemag.org/content/359/6380/1146.

18. "Gettysburg National Cemetery, Gettysburg, Pennsylvania," National Park Service, accessed May 22, 2019, https://www.nps.gov/nr/travel/national_cemeteries/pennsylvania/gettysburg_national_cemetery.html.

19. "Gettysburg Address Hay Draft," Library of Congress, accessed May 22, 2019, https://www.loc.gov/exhibits/gettysburg-address/ext/trans-hay-draft.html.

20. Trip Gabriel, "A Timeline of Steve King's Racist Remarks and Divisive Actions," *New York Times*, January 15, 2019, www.newyorktimes.com/2019/01/15/us/politics/steve-king-offensive-quotes.html.

21. House Resolution 41: Rejecting White Nationalism and White Supremacy, US House of Representatives, 116th Congress, January 15, 2019. https://congress.gov/bill/116th-congress/house-resolution/41/text.

22. Vivian Cho, "How Science and Genetics Are Reshaping the Race Debate of the 21st Century," Science in the News, April 17, 2017, http://sitn.hms.harvard.edu/flash/2017/science-genetics-reshaping-race-debate-21st-cantury/.

23. "Statistical Abstract of the United States 1973," US Department of Commerce, accessed May 22, 2019, https://www2.census.gov/library/publications/1973/compendia/statab/94ed/1973-01.pdf?#.

24. "Quick Facts, United States," Bureau of the Census, accessed May 22, 2019, https://www.census.gov/quickfacts/fact/table/US/PST045218.

25. "World Merchandise Exports," World Bank, accessed May 22, 2019, https://data.worldbank.org/indicator/tx.val.mrch.cd.wt.

26. Maureen A. Craig, Julian M. Rucker, and Jennifer A. Richeson, "The Pitfalls and Promise of Increasing Racial Diversity: Threat, Contact, and Race Relations

in the 21st Century," *Current Directions in Psychological Science*, December 19, 2017, 188–93.

27. Ronald Reagan, "Remarks at the Presentation Ceremony for the Presidential Medal of Freedom," Ronald Reagan Presidential Library and Museum, January 19, 1989, https://www.reaganlibrary.gov/011989b.

28. "Map of Human Migration," Genographic Project, National Geographic, accessed May 22, 2019, https://genographic.nationalgeographic.com/human-journey/.

29. Rock and Grant, "Why Diverse Teams Are Smarter."

30. "The Responsibilities of Citizenship," Pew Research Center, April 26, 2018, https://people-press.org/2018/04/26/9-the-responsibilities-of-citizenship/.

31. Claire Andre and Manuel Velasquez, "Creating the Good Society," Markkula Center for Applied Ethics, Santa Clara University, accessed May 22, 2019, https://www.scu.edu/ethics/ethics-resources/ethical-decision-making/creating-the-good-society/.

32. Steven Levitsky and Daniel Ziblatt, *How Democracies Die* (New York: Crown 2018), 101.

CONCLUSION

1. "Representative John Lewis Commemorates 50th Anniversary of the Civil Rights Act," Congressman John Lewis, July 2, 2014, https://johnlewis.house.gov/media-center/press-releases/rep-john-lewis-commemorates-50th-anniversary-civil-rights-act.

INDEX

Abramoff, Jack, 65
Americans with Disabilities Act (ADA), 17–18
Andre, Claire, 119–20
Aristotle, 10–11, 22, 43, 52, 124

Bayh, Birch, 109
BEA. *See* Budget Enforcement Act
behavioral ethics, 45–46
Beloved Community, 123
bias: behavioral ethics research on, 45–46; conformity, 46; gender, 48; news programs influencing, 20; personal, 46–47, 48–49; unconscious, 48–49
Bill of Rights, 28, 37, 52
bin Laden, Osama, 40
Blagojevich, Rod, 42–43
blind trusts, 74
Branson, Richard, 56
bribery, 65, 80
Brokaw, Tom, 10
Budget Enforcement Act (BEA), 39–40
Buffett, Warren, 97
Bush, George H. W.: ADA supported by, 17; BEA of, 39–40; Commission

on Federal Ethics Law Reform established by, 72
business: code of ethics in, 97–99; macroethics in, 89–95; microethics in, 95–101

campaign finance, 83–86
Cantwell, Maria, 51
capitalism: macroethics and, 89–95; market economy and, 12–13; microethics and, 95–101; social value of, 91–92
caring: for democracy, 106; patriotism in connection with, 117–19; as pillar of character, 19–20
carrots and sticks metaphor, 93–94
CEOs. *See* chief executive officers
character: caring as pillar of, 19–20; challenges to building, 34–35; citizenship as pillar of, 20; commitment to ethics and, 6; Constitution defining American, 36–37; as decisive factor in life, 1; as destiny, 5, 31–32; fairness as pillar of, 18–19; Josephson Institute of Ethics identifying pillars of, 16; leadership and, 40–49; meaning of, 10–15;

patriotism and, 107–21; pillars of, 16–20, 107–21; power and, 105; purpose driven by, 53–57; reputation in relation to, 39; respect as pillar of, 17–18; responsibility as pillar of, 18; strength from, 26–34; trustworthiness as pillar of, 16–17; universal values and, 15

chief executive officers (CEOs): facial characteristics and competence of, 48; as Level 5 leaders, 40–41, 99–100, 111; salary growth for, 95

children: caring for, 19–20; of Great Depression, 59; moral development of, 41

CIO. See Congress of Industrial Organizations

citizens/citizenship: ethics, 105–6; gratitude for, 8; integrity of, 15, 63–64; leadership assessment by, 77; patriotism in connection with, 119–21; as pillar of character, 20

civil rights legislation, 17–18

civil rights movement, 20, 103–5

civility, 111–12

Clinton, William J. (Bill), 74

Clinton, Hillary, 74

code of ethics: in business, 97–99; in Congress, 78–81; in Executive Branch, 68–78; in Judicial Branch, 81–83; pillars of character integrated into, 107–21; purpose of government employee, 66–68

Collins, Jim, 40–41, 99, 111

Commission on Federal Ethics Law Reform, 72

communism, 12

community: beloved, 123; democratic, 103; relationship building within, 27–28; veterans as foundation of, 9–10

conflicts of interest: in Congress, 80–81; Constitution on financial, 76–77; democracy undermined by, 64–65, 70–71; financial disclosure state-

ments and, 68–69, 74; lobbyist practices as, 2; Postal Service and GSA violating, 75

conformity bias, 46

Congress: ADA supported by, 17; conflicts of interest and exploitation in, 80–81; constitutional requirements for, 27; gifts for, 1–2, 65; gift restrictions for, 78, 79–80; salary raises for, 78–79

Congress of Industrial Organizations (CIO), 85

congressional district maps, 86–87

Congressional Ethics Reform Act, 78

Constitution: American character defined by, 36–37; Bill of Rights, 28, 37, 52; Congress requirements from, 27; defense of, 77; discrimination undermining, 8; Fifteenth Amendment of, 12, 17; on financial conflicts of interest, 76–77; First Amendment of, 24, 27; Fourteenth Amendment of, 17; fundamentals of character established in, 11–12; Nineteenth Amendment of, 12; purpose from, 52; Sixth Amendment of, 71, 81; transparency required by, 27, 37, 71; Twenty-Seventh Amendment of, 79; Twenty-Sixth Amendment of, 109

conventional morality, 41–42, 43

corporate social responsibility, 89–92, 95, 101

corruption: economic growth impacted by, 5–6, 30–31; by lobbyists, 65

courage: development of, 43–44; embodiment of patriotism and, 9–10

"Creating the Good Society," 119–20

debt responsibility, 18

decision-making: with character, 39–49; diversity improving, 111, 124; steps for ethical, 57–61

Declaration of Independence: discrimination undermining, 8; fundamentals of character established in, 11–12

deficit reduction, 39–40

democracy: Beloved Community and, 123; caring for, 106; conflicts of interest undermining, 64–65, 70–71; definition of, 70; dishonesty undermining, 4–5; ethics as fundamental to, 1–8; key to ethical behavior and stronger, 35–36; liberty of, 89; microethics and protecting, 24–26; origin of, 12; promise of, 51; responsibility of protecting, 105

democratic community, 103

deontology theory, 44

Department of Defense, 53

Department of Health and Human Services, 54

Department of State, 53, 55

destiny, 5, 31–32

dictatorship, 12

discrimination: gender, 17, 109–10; principles undermined by, 8

dishonesty: consequences of, 108–9; democracy undermined by, 4–5

diversity: in decision-making, 111, 124; racial, 116–17; value of, 118

doctors, 34–35

Duckworth, Tammy, 18

economic growth: corruption impacting, 5–6, 30–31; FDR strategies for, 29–30; income inequality impacting, 13

Eisenhower, Dwight D., 9

Eli Lilly and Company, 54, 55

emotions. *See* feelings/emotions

ethical behavior: benefits of, 51; Fourteen Principles of Ethical Conduct on, 72–73, 75–76; key to, 35–36; meaning of, 20–24

ethical decision-making, 57–61

ethics: behavioral, 45–46; citizen, 105–6; commitment to character and, 6; concerns with leadership, 3; definition of, 23, 60; deontology theory of, 44; federal elections and, 83–88; as fundamentals of democracy, 1–8; macroethics, 23–24, 89–95; microethics, 23–26, 95–101; principles protected with, 14; utilitarian theory of, 45; virtue theory of, 43–44. *See also* code of ethics

Ethics in Government Act (1978), 65–66

European Recovery Program, 30

Executive Branch, 68–78. *See also* presidents

exploitation, 80–81

fairness: in Judicial Branch, 81–83; patriotism in connection with, 115–17; as pillar of character, 18–19; responsibility to, 3

Farm Credit Administration (FCA), 43, 68–69

FDIC. *See* Federal Deposit Insurance Corporation

FDR. *See* Roosevelt, Franklin D.

Federal Deposit Insurance Corporation (FDIC), 97–99

federal elections: campaign finance in, 83–86; congressional district maps influencing, 86–87; Russian intervention in, 112–13; voter suppression in, 87–88

feelings/emotions: behavioral ethics research on, 45–46; ethics in relation to, 22

Fifteenth Amendment, 12, 17

finance, campaign, 83–86

financial deregulation, 96–97

financial disclosure statements: conflicts of interest and, 68–69, 74; laws on, 65–66

financial interests, 7, 73–74, 76–77
First Amendment, 24, 27
Ford, Gerald, 74
Fourteen Principles of Ethical Conduct, 72–73, 75–76
Fourteenth Amendment, 17
free press, 24–25, 27
free speech, 24, 27
Friedman, Milton, 89–91, 100–101

Gallup polls, 5, 52, 59
gender bias, 48
gender discrimination, 17, 109–10
General Services Administration (GSA), 75
Gettysburg address, 70, 115–16
gifts: for Congress, 1–2, 65; for doctors, 34–35; restrictions on, 78, 79–80
Gini index, 94
globalization, 118
good neighbor policy, 29–30
gratitude, 8
Great Depression, 19–20, 29, 59, 99
Greatest Generation, The (Brokaw), 10
Great Recession, 95–96, 99
GSA. *See* General Services Administration

Hamilton, Lee H., v
Harkin, Tom, 17
Hawking, Stephen, 33–34
Heraclitus, 5
honesty: for building trust, 31; responsibility for, 44. *See also* dishonesty
Hosmer, LaRue, 57

income inequality: economic growth impacted by, 13; Gini index for measuring, 94; unionization for reducing, 94–95

information literacy, 114–15
inspiration: research, 7–8; for self-governance, 11
integrity: of citizens, 15, 63–64; embodiment of, 31; as essence of morality, 21; importance of, 4; leadership, 63–64; trust from, 5–6, 52

Jim Crow laws, 104
Josephson Institute of Ethics, 16
journalism, 24–25, 27
Judges Code of Conduct, 82
Judicial Branch: code of ethics in, 81–83; presidents attacking, 113

Kant, Immanuel, 44
Kaptur, Marcy, xi
Kellogg Company, 19–20, 54, 55
Kennedy, John F., 63, 88
Kimberly-Clark Corporation, 99–100
King, Martin Luther, Jr., 51
King, Steve, 116
Kohlberg, Lawrence, 41–42
Korean War veterans, 9–10

laws: on campaign finance restrictions, 84–85; conflicts of interest classified by, 64–65; ethics in relation to, 22; financial deregulation, 96–97; financial disclosure statement, 65–66
leadership: character and, 40–49; concerns with ethical, 3; integrity, 63–64; Level 5, 40–41, 99–100, 111; responsibility of assessing, 77
Legislative Branch. *See* Congress
Level 5 leaders, 40–41, 99–100, 111
Lewis, John, 20, 123, 124
liberty, 89
Lincoln, Abraham: on character and power, 105; on character and reputa-

tion, 39; Gettysburg address of, 70, 115–16
lobbyists, 1–2, 65, 79

macroethics: in business, 89–95; definition and examples of, 23–24
Madison, James, 79
market economy, 12–13
Marshall, George C., 30
Mastering Civility (Porath), 111–12
medical prescription study, 34–35
microethics: in business, 95–101; definition and examples of, 23–24; protection of democracy and, 24–26
Microsoft, 54, 55
Mill, John Stuart, 12
minorities: Constitutional Amendments on rights of, 12, 17; population growth of, 116–17; racism toward, 116; sentencing issues for, 82
mission statements, 53–57
monarchy, 12
morality: characteristics of, 22; definitions of, 20–21; development levels of, 41–43; theories, 43–45

Nineteenth Amendment, 12

Obama, Barack, 40, 68, 74
Operation Neptune Spear, 40

PACs. *See* political action committees
Paper International Hall of Fame, 100
patriotism: caring in connection with, 117–19; citizenship in connection with, 119–21; embodiment of courage and, 9–10; fairness in connection with, 115–17; respect in connection with, 109–12; responsibility in con-

nection with, 112–15; trustworthiness in connection with, 107–9
Pentagon Papers, 104
personal bias, 46–47, 48–49
pharmaceutical companies, 34–35
political action committees (PACs), 85–86, 115
Porath, Christine, 111–12
Postal Service, 75
postconventional morality, 42
power: abuse of, 106; of citizens, 105–6; of democracy, 51; trappings of, 2–3
preconventional morality, 41, 42–43
presidential election (2016), 112–13
presidents: dishonesty among, 4; financial interests of, 7, 73–74, 76–77; Judicial Branch attacked by, 113; tax returns released by, 69. *See also specific presidents*
principles: discrimination undermining, 8; ethics protecting, 14; privileges over, 9
privileges, 9
purpose: character-driven, 53–57; from Constitution, 52; of employee code of ethics, 66–68

racial diversity, 116–17
racism, 116
Randolph, A. Philip, 103, 105
Reagan, Ronald, 118
Reciprocal Trade Agreement Act (RTAA), 29
relationship building, 27–28
religion, 22
reputation, 39
research inspiration, 7–8
respect: loss of, 108; patriotism in connection with, 109–12; as pillar of character, 17–18

responsibility: to fairness, 3; for honesty, 44; of leadership assessment, 77; patriotism in connection with, 112–15; as pillar of character, 18; of protecting democracy, 105; in self-governance, 106; sharing of, 123–24; social, 89–92, 95, 101

Rockefeller, Nelson, 74

Roosevelt, Franklin D. (FDR): CIO support for, 85; good neighbor policy of, 29–30; on liberty of democracy, 89

Roosevelt, Theodore, 1

RTAA. *See* Reciprocal Trade Agreement Act

Russian intervention, 112–13

salaries: CEO growth in, 95; Congress raising own, 78–79

scandals, 32–33

self-governance: Constitution as foundation of, 11; responsibility in, 106

Sentencing Commission, 82

Sixth Amendment, 71, 81

Smith, Darwin E., 99–100

social media, 114–15

social responsibility, 89–92, 95, 101

social value, 91–92

socialism, 12

standard of living, 89, 90

Starbucks, 19

State Integrity Investigation, 6

Stop Trading on Congressional Knowledge Act (2012), 66

Sullenberger, Chesley, 16–17

Tax Cuts and Jobs Act (2017), 108

tax return disclosure, 68–69, 74

Title IX, 17, 109–10

tolerance, 117

totalitarian government, 12

transparency: Constitution requiring, 27, 37, 71; financial disclosure statements for, 65–66, 68–69, 74; trustworthiness demanding, 107–8

truth: information literacy development and, 114–15; of liberty and democracy, 89

trust/trustworthiness: honesty for building, 31; from integrity, 5–6, 52; patriotism in connection with, 107–9; as pillar of character, 16–17; scandals and loss of, 32–33

Twenty-Seventh Amendment, 79

Twenty-Sixth Amendment, 109

unconscious bias, 48–49

unionization, 94–95

universal values, 15

utilitarian theory, 45

Velasquez, Manuel, 119–20

veterans: in Congress, 80–81; as foundation of community, 9–10; mistreatment of, 104

vice presidents, 73–74

Vietnam War, 4, 103–5

Virginia House of Burgesses, 83–84

virtue: Aristotle on, 10–11, 22, 43, 52, 124; moral development in relation to, 42; theory, 43–44

voter suppression: in federal elections, 87–88; as form of disrespect, 109

voters: concerns with seriousness of, 5; Constitutional Amendments on rights of, 12, 17, 109; female candidate skepticism from, 47, 48; registration help for, 27–28. *See also* federal elections

Washington, George, 83–84

Watergate, 4

Wells Fargo, 16

white supremacy/nationalism, 116

Winfrey, Oprah, 55–56

women: Constitutional Amendments on rights of, 12, 17; sentencing inconsistencies with, 82–83; Title IX impacting, 17, 109–10; voter skepticism of, 47, 48

workforce: children engaged in, 19; diversity, 118; income inequality, 13, 94–95; unionization, 94–95

World War II, 9–10, 28–30

Yale University study, 2

JILL LONG THOMPSON is a college professor and public servant with a long history of advancing reform in professional ethics. She is a former Member of Congress who served three terms representing northeast Indiana in the US House. She has also served as an Under Secretary at the US Department of Agriculture and as Board Chair and CEO of the Farm Credit Administration.

While serving in the House, Long Thompson introduced legislation restricting the acceptance of gifts by Members of Congress, and she led the Farm Credit Administration Board to adopt a policy that strengthened the agency's arm's-length provisions pertaining to its relationship with the institutions it regulates.

Dr. Long Thompson grew up on a family farm in rural Whitley County, Indiana, and first became interested in government when her dad became a precinct committeeman with the county Democratic Party. Her understanding of the democratic process began at age six when she accompanied her mother going door-to-door to register voters in their township, with the goal of generating support for a neighbor who was running for county sheriff. When he won the office, she began to understand that democracy is a shared responsibility and that one person can make a difference.

As someone who came of age during the civil rights movement, the Vietnam War, and the Watergate break-in, she also became very aware of the important role integrity plays in democracy. And she began to understand how unethical behavior can undermine democratic principles and threaten a democratic society. She believes the people, as well as those who hold public office, are responsible for ensuring our government is run with integrity, fairness, and transparency.

Jill Long Thompson is a Visiting Clinical Associate Professor and Dean's Fellow for the Intersection of Business and Government at Indiana University Bloomington where she teaches ethics at the Kelley School of Business and the O'Neill School of Public and Environmental Affairs. She holds the PhD and the MBA from Indiana University Bloomington and a BS in Business from Valparaiso University. She lives with her husband, Don, a retired fighter pilot and airline captain, on their farm in Marshall County, Indiana.